About the author.

Jason Blake has always loved bars, starting with his well-spent youth in a pub called The Bell Inn. Drinking alongside friends, Blake finds that bars and pubs offer comfort, a place in which to relax and feel most like himself.

In rich and colourful writing, which brims with insight and wisdom, he brings to life some 30 years of experience by encapsulating it in an easy to read format for future generations of drinkers. So, How To Be Professional Drinker is as much a handbook as it is a love letter to alcohol, the bars, pubs and clubs that have been Blake's sanctuary, and a celebration of drinking, friendship and freedom that is drinking culture at its very best.

"I just love drinking and being drunk."
JASON BLAKE

THE
HANDBOOK
HOW TO BE A
PROFESSIONAL
DRINKER

WRITTEN & DESIGNED BY JASON BLAKE

BRAD,
" HAPPY DRINKING ! "
JB

First published in Great Britain 2016 by 'You Know!'™

Copyright © Jason Blake 2016.
The author has asserted his moral rights.

A CIP catalogue record for this title is available from the British Library.

ISBN 978-0-9955298-0-9

Printed and bound in Rotherham, Great Britain from sustainable sources. FSC Accredited.

Introduction.

DRINKING IS EASY. DRINKING LIKE A PROFESSIONAL IS A SKILL. IF YOU DRINK, AND LIKE TO HAVE A GOOD TIME, THEN HOW TO BE A PROFESSIONAL DRINKER **IS DEFINITELY THE HANDBOOK FOR YOU.**

Dedicated to: *The very best of times.* ||||||||||||||||||||||||||||||||||||||||||||||||||||||||||||||||||||||||||||||||||||||||||||||||||||

Index.

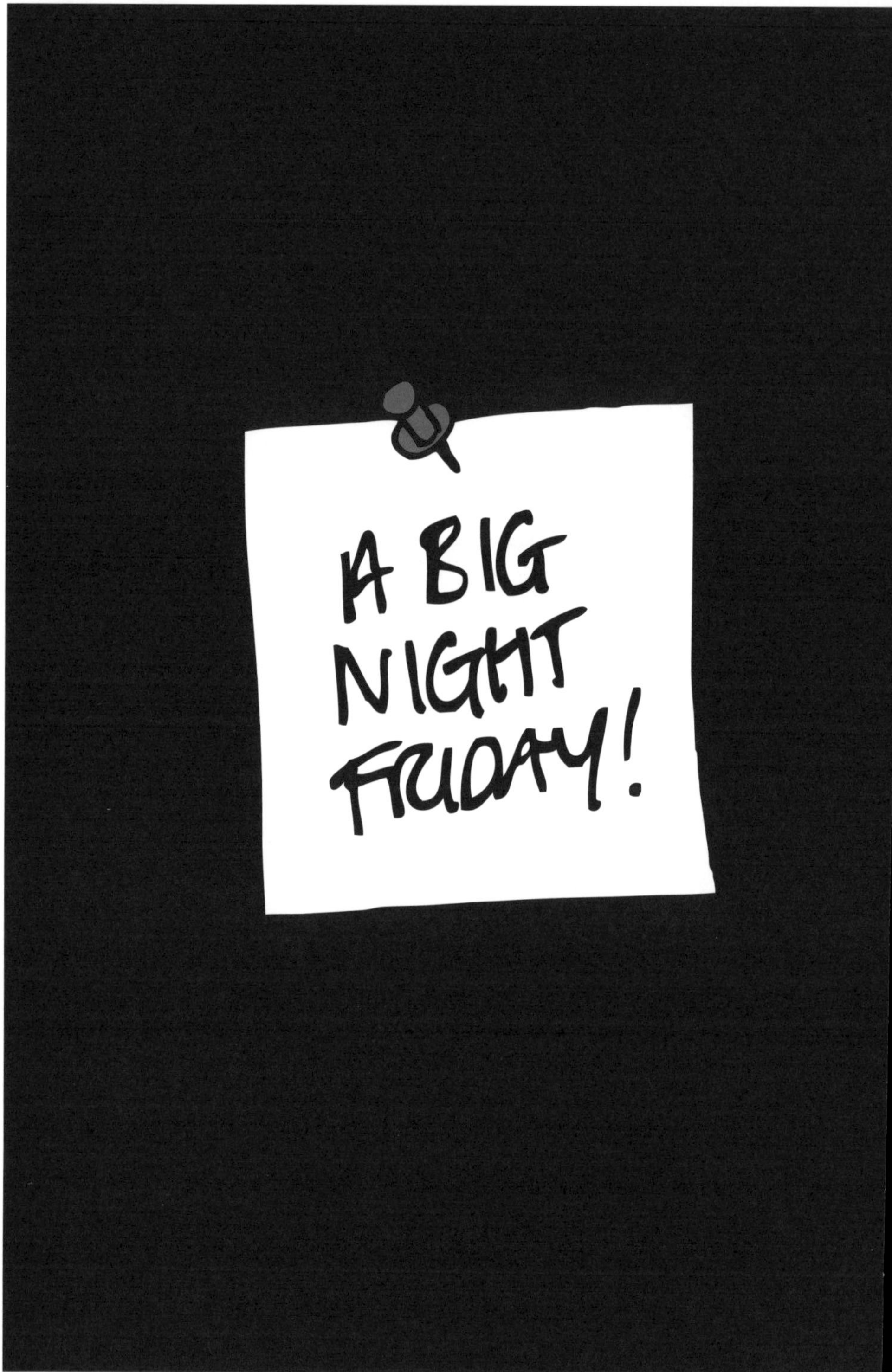
A BIG
NIGHT
FRIDAY!

BEING A PROFESSIONAL.

Definition of Professional Drinker:
A person who can handle a vast quantity and mix of alcohol over an extensive period without ever having anybody take care of them.

'You're either in or you're out!'

A word to the wise.

Wander into any pub, bar or club on a Friday or Saturday night and you'll see an abundance of amateur drinkers.

They start their night out with eager smiles and bags of energy, but these drinkers will end up lying in piss soaked doorways, covered in their own vomit, slumped in a police cell or wind up in A&E battered and bruised. These amateurs ruin it for the rest of us who seek relaxation, freedom and merriment.

If you're one of them, and you want your nights out to become more fun, put pay to mornings of head pain and unsettled stomachs, find out how to avoid shame, injury, a police record and even a broken relationship. There's no need to give up the excesses of alcohol, this handbook is here to help.

A professional drinker.

'Professional drinker' is a colloquial term for someone who can handle his or her drink. In terms of The Handbook it also advises the importance of being professional in your attitude, knowledge and experience.

Vision, aim and mission.

VISION.
There is a fine line between being a professional and an alcoholic. This handbook will show you, and teach you, the difference. Drinking for social enjoyment and fun, not that of dependency.

AIM.
To gain a good grounding and understanding of all aspects of alcohol, and that of a great night out. Alongside being able to perform in this environment at an optimum and sustainable level for longer, as well as eliminate the woes of recovery.

MISSION.
To become a professional drinker.

|||||||||||||||||||||||||||||||||||||||||||||||||||||||||||||||||||||||||||||||||||||||||||||||||||||||||||||||||||||||||||||||

It's a risky business.

HEALTH.

Alcohol beyond moderation is a health risk. The current UK government guidelines for both men and women is not to regularly exceed more than 14 units of alcohol per week. Alcohol miss use can cause a variety of health problems; *In the short term these include antisocial behaviour, injury, unsafe sex, loss of possessions and alcohol poisoning. In the long-term it can lead to heart disease, stroke, liver disease, liver cancer and bowel cancer as well as social problems; unemployment, divorce, domestic abuse and homelessness.

*Source information NHS, 2013. NHS Choices, London: NHS.
Available from: www.nhs.uk/conditions/Alcohol-misuse/Pages/Introduction.aspx [Accessed 1 August 2015].

ABILITY.

Alcohol can impair your ability to drive or operate machinery.

DEATH.

Accept that you could well die, you need to see that it's a risky vocation like that of any extreme sport. I hope that when I pass they'll say 'Here's to a great drinker!' And the last drink will be on me.

DISCLAIMER.

You must be over 18 years of age to purchase and read this publication. This handbook is a guide for those that drink to get drunk and to better help them have more fun and come to less harm than they otherwise would.

|||||||||||||||||||||||||||||||||||||||||||||||||||||||||||||||||||||||||||||||||||||||||||||||||||||||||||||||||||||||||||||||

A little bit of history.

From the Neolithic era, hunter-gatherers, to civilisation, nations and modern times alcohol has been produced and consumed by humans.

GLOBAL TREND.

The global market for alcoholic beverages is huge in terms of consumption, revenue and taxes, which out way any negative costs in the majority of countries. Has it always been like this? The answer is of course yes, and in population terms we drank way more in the past than we do now. This may well have been down to it being safer to drink than water, but it seems humans have inherently loved and bonded with alcohol ever since its creation. Let's have a look at a little bit of history.

7000 B.C.

Wine jars dating back to ancient China, 7000 B.C, show that wine was being produced by fermenting fruit, rice and honey.

4000 B.C.

Egyptian paintings from around 4000 B.C also depicted how they created wines. As well as signs, that like bread, beer was seen as one of the foods of life, made daily it was a stable in their diet.

2700 B.C.

Around 2700 B.C the Babylonians worshiped wine gods / goddesses. They adored wine and beer, making offerings while they drank.

3000 B.C. - 2000 B.C.

Between 3000 B.C. and 2000 B.C. alcoholic drinks produced from rice were made in India. While carvings in Native America depict they had beer very close to the ones we have today.

Since the dawn of man, and the emergence of civilisation alcohol has been a part of all cultures around the world. Whether it has been for medicine, courage, celebrations, to honour or to seduce… it's here to stay.

RULE BRITANNIA.

It is hard to put a finger on why us Brits love alcohol so much. Some 12,000 years ago during the Neolithic period Stone Age beer jugs indicate that we were fermenting alcohol from as early as the 8th Century. This mainly being due to water supplies being polluted by sewerage. Drinks like cider, ale and mead became popular in lower class society.

Then came the abuse; first recorded during the Industrial Revolution in the 18th century. All controls, albeit informal, in regards to alcohol consumption broke down as people from rural and urban slums were brought together for hard manual labour combined with long hours. This also happened at a time when new and better ways of producing alcohol developed; with the distillation of juniper berries it made for 60% proof gin. With no regulations it wasn't long before gin was the answer to mentally escaping the tough factory work and poor living conditions.

The government swiftly brought in the gin law in 1736 to try and curb consumption yet it had very much the opposite effect as people rebelled by drinking more, protesting and even rioting.

'Betterment' however became the new agenda. With further legal reforms a new respect was established with temperance soon being supported by the middle classes. Heavy drinking was no longer seen as just a bad habit but reprehensible and that of weakness. It was a strong movement but fell short of American prohibition, which actually outlawed the sale of alcohol in the early 1900s.

Despite this, a firm foothold of traditional heavy feast-like drinking patterns remained… 'Fine wine, fine mead, fine friends' and it still remains in our culture today.

NORTHERN EUROPE AS A WHOLE.
Northern European drinking culture was one of extremes, from spells of complete abstinence to heavy bouts of drinking, the later of which has been inherited today. In the UK it's almost seen as traditional behaviour to get really drunk, thus making it more acceptable, regardless of any government directive on health, social issues or their attempts at control through taxation.

CONCLUSION.
Alcohol is a psychoactive drug commonly used for its intoxicating effects throughout history, as well as today and no doubt the future.

'Fine wine, fine mead, fine friends!'

In William Hogarth's 1751 engravings 'Beer Street' and 'Gin Lane' *(Overleaf)* he illustrates the alcohol-fuelled mayhem of the time.

William Hogarth's 1751 engraving 'Gin Lane'.

THE DRINKS.

Alcoholic beverages are divided into three categories; beers, wines and spirits.

Beers.

BEER.

Dating as far back as the early Neolithic period (circa 4000 B.C.), when grains were first farmed, beer is one of the oldest alcoholic drinks. Beer is produced either from malted barley (generally), cereal grain or malted wheat by the saccharification of starch and fermentation of the derived sugar. The addition of hops is used to add flavour, bitterness as well as a natural preservative. Fruits and herbs can also be added to create or enhance flavour.

Practically any substance that comprises of sugar can produce a sweet liquid that given time will ferment to formulate alcohol. It's highly probable that cultures, in separation from one another, would have discovered quite swiftly how they could acquire this liquid from starch and therefore devised beer. Along with bread, beer increased prosperity and has long been credited for giving humans time for development and technology, therefore instrumental in the creation and achievement of civilisations.

Nations that have a strong beer drinking culture have so as part of their heritage and traditions. This usually involves feast drinking (celebrations), beer festivals and a rich pub culture. These social outlets often include small events; quizzes, live music and activities such as skittles, darts and pool. Throughout the world beer is largely manufactured to be around 4% to 6% ABV, although there are a number of much stronger examples in recent years. In modern times it is mainly served cold, warm beer not being as refreshing. On the flip side there is even alcohol-free beer, but I'm not sure what that's for?!

CIDER.

Dating back to around 1300 B.C. cider is an alcoholic drink made by fermenting apple juice. Almost every variety or mix of apple juice can be used to create cider, which makes for such a good range of flavours. In addition to this there are other comparable fruit based drinks such as pear perry (often referred to as pear cider today).

The UK is one of the biggest producers and consumers of cider in the world. It is particularly favoured in the south west and east of England. The ABV ranges from 1.2% to around 8.5% with some more traditional English ciders being that bit stronger.

PALE ALE.

Using mostly pale malt and top fermenting yeast, pale ale is one of the key beers throughout the world.

STOUT.

Using slow fermenting yeast, stout is produced and brewed from roasted malts, or barley. It tends to be very dark with a creamy head, which is dependent on brand as well as variations of stout; dry stout, imperial stout and Baltic porter.

||||||||||||||||||||||||||||||||||||||||||||||||||||||||||||||||||||||||||||||||||||||||||||||||||||||||||||||||||||||||||||||||||||||||||||||||||||||||||

MILD ALE.
Rich in colour, mild has a very malty taste. There are lighter and stronger varieties, however the usual ABV is between 3 to 3.6%.

WHEAT BEER.
Brewed with wheat it also has a sizeable amount of malted barley. There is much variable flavour with wheat beers as it greatly depends on its style.

LAGER.
Lager is the world's most popular beer. Brewed and fermented in cool conditions it mellows and becomes free of residue, preventing natural esters and other unrequired elements that makes for its clear, refreshing and crisp taste.

LAMBIC.
Naturally fermented using wild yeast as apposed to cultivated yeasts. Lambic is a popular Belgium beer.

REAL ALE.
Produced from traditional ingredients real ale is brewed and then matured by secondary fermentation where it is distributed and provided using no additional carbon dioxide.

BEER GLASSES.
It goes without saying that the British pint is important, but what is also just as important is what it is consumed from, and there are many styles of glass. The classic dimpled beer mug is one of my favourites, unfortunately it's prone to spillage when very drunk as your grip becomes less firm, enabling the glass to sit at a 45 degree angle. With this in mind the best glass by far for keeping steady is the tulip (see the Drinkware guide on page 77).

Wines.

The history of wine dates back centuries, we have currently traced it back to c 6000 B.C. in Georgia, giving wine such an expansive history, with significant importance in religion. Ancient Egyptians linked red wine with blood, believing it to be the blood of those who had battled against the gods.

Wine is produced from grapes (or other fermented fruits), which have the perfect chemical make up to ferment without having to add nutrients such as sugar, enzymes, acids or even water. The sugar content in grapes is consumed by yeast, which turns into alcohol and carbon dioxide. Different types of yeast and grapes, alongside intricate interaction and reactions during fermentation, including that of human adjustment produces a huge array of different wines. The basic categories of wine are white, rosé, red and sparkling, and usually referenced thereafter by the name of the product with which they are made, examples are rice wine, fruit wine and barley wine.

||||||||||||||||||||||||||||||||||||||||||||||||||||||||||||||||||||||||||||||||||||||||||||||||||||||||||||||||||||||||||||||||||||||||||||||||||||||||||

Liqueurs.

Descending from herbal medicines by Monks in Italy around the 13th century, liqueurs were produced from a distilled spirit. They are flavoured with fruit, flowers, nuts, herbs, spices and cream. Usually sweet tasting as further sugar, or sweetener, is added. Once mixed a set time is allowed for the flavours to blend sufficiently.

Made the world over, liqueurs are formally drank at the end of a meal. They can be drank neat (usually with ice), with cream, added to coffee or mixed with other spirits, juice or carbonated drinks to make many different cocktails. Liqueurs are also often used in cooking.

Spirits.

Spirits like whisky, rum or vodka are distilled and initially brewed from fermented fruit, plant juice or a starch from grain(s). Distilled spirit (or liquor) has a much higher ABV than that of beer or wine.

VODKA.

Vodka is created from the distillation of fermented grains or potatoes and is largely water and ethanol with the addition of flavourings (fruits and sugar are often used in modern vodkas). The two countries renowned for vodka are Russia and Poland. They tend to differ in that the finer Russian vodkas are made from wheat while the Polish favour rye mash.

The name vodka comes from the phrase 'to burn' due to the harshness of its initial form. Flavours were added to disguise this making it much easier to consume. Popular in Eastern Europe; Russia, Ukraine, Poland, Lithuania, Latvia, Estonia and the Czech Republic vodka has been distilled to around 40% to 50% ABV and is traditionally drank neat.

In the 1940s vodka became popular globally where its use is primarily in mixed drinks and cocktails like Black Russian, Bloody Mary, Screwdriver… the list goes on, and on, as vodka is arguably the best neutral spirit. These days vodka has once again introduced flavours, only this time as brand extensions, offering more variety, increasing its popularity even further.

GIN.

One of the most popular spirits, gin is produced with its main flavour derived from juniper berries. Originating as a herbal medicine in the early middle ages, it has evolved to become more refined over the centuries so we now have a wide variety of gins in terms of style, flavour and origin.

There are references to gin (genever) dating as far back as the 13th century. In 1585 when the British assisted Antwerp against the Spanish, much was drank for its calming effects and is most likely the source of the phrase 'Dutch courage'. In the first half of the 18th Century gin shops appeared throughout England, particularly London, as the government allowed unlicensed production, an era which is referred to as the 'Gin Craze'. Social problems soon arose, as the price of gin, like beer, was favourable to the poor.

Although negative phrases such as 'gin-soaked' (drunk) and 'mother's ruin' (gin) still linger on gin is seen today as a more sophisticated drink. Gaining popularity over the last few years gin bars are on the increase... maybe it's time to start my gin library.

SLOE GIN.

Originating from gin being blended with blackthorn fruit (sloe). Today it's primarily produced using a neutral spirit and flavourings. Other varieties are available which use fruits such as plums or damsons.

WHISK(E)Y.

Typically stored / aged in wooden barrels (charred white oak in the main) whisky is produced from fermented grain mash. Numerous grains such as rye, malted rye, barley, malted barley, wheat, buckwheat and corn are used to create different varieties of whisky.

Whisky, (like wine) has many types and classes:

Bourbon whiskey - produced from mash comprising of no less than 51% corn (maize)
Corn whiskey - produced from mash comprising of no less than 80% corn
Malt whisky - produced from mash comprising of no less than 51% malted barley

Rye whiskey - produced from mash comprising of no less than 51% rye
Rye malt whiskey - produced from mash comprising of no less than 51% malted rye
Wheat whiskey - produced from mash comprising of no less than 51% wheat
Blended whisky - a combination of separate whiskeys blended together that may also include neutral spirit, colouring and flavourings.

In addition to the varieties of grains, different characteristics are produced through the distillation process, varying aging and barrels to create different types and classes. The very first whiskeys, much like vodka, were very harsh and over the centuries have been refined to become much smoother.

SCOTCH WHISKY.
The Highland, Lowland, Campbeltown, Speyside and Islay are key areas in which Scottish whisky is made. Malt and grain are mixed to produce blends with peat smoke often used to create the distinct flavour of Scotch.

AGING.
The period between distillation and bottling is classed as the 'age' and defines the time in which the barrel has reacted and infused with the whiskey, adjusting to its final flavour. The aging process is refined for quality of flavour; therefore whiskies that are older (aged longer) may not actually be better than a younger whisky. A whisky that has been bottled for many years will usually only be expensive due to its rarity rather than that of taste.

AMERICAN BOURBON.
America has a strong affiliation with whiskey; it even used it as currency during the American Revolution between 1765 and 1783. From 1920 to 1933 all sales of alcohol were prohibited throughout the country and thereafter became known as the Prohibition era. However, during this period whiskey had a federal dispensation and could be prescribed by a licensed doctor or pharmacy.

'There's no such thing as a bad whisky... it's just that some are better than others.'

|||||||||||||||||||||||||||||||||||||||||||||||||||||||||||||||||||||||||||||||||||||||||||||||||||||||||||||||||||||||||||||||||||||||||||||

A SPECIAL NOD TO GUINNESS. (STOUT)

Guinness is a great drink and I have loved it for many years. However, its downside is that it's a heavy drink and can bloat you, therefore hold you back. It's like a meal in a glass and you can easily get deceived by this, often joking as if it is non-alcoholic, 'I don't understand why I went nude and shoved that item up my arse I was only drinking Guinness?!' the mind boggles. The best advice is to use a few pints of Guinness to line your stomach early on, and always look to drink it in the right pub / bar where it's popular in order to get a decent / good pint.

IT'S ALL MIXED UP THESE DAYS.

Such is our love for alcohol that beyond beer, wine and the standard spirits we have hundreds of milder liquors as well as stronger spirits like Stroh 80 (80% ABV). We love to be inventive with flavours as we mix and create thousands of sophisticated cocktails and punches, to the ready mixed, and cheap, bottled alco-pops to get our younger generation started on the road to the joys of alcohol.

See the chapter What Would You Like To Drink? on page 59 for some of the best and my personal favourite shots, short drinks, long drinks, cocktails and punches.

Alcohol is legally produced, sold and consumed in nearly every country in the world, many of which having laws to enable regulation and high taxation.

|||||||||||||||||||||||||||||||||||||||||||||||||||||||||||||||||||||||||||||||||||||||||||||||||||||||||||||||||||||||||||||||||||||||||||||

24 | The Drinks

DRINKING.

Developing the right
grounding and mindset
for drinking.

'Aim to be a happy drunk!'

The stages of intoxication.

SOCIABLE. (Guidance 4-5 Units)
After just a few drinks the alcohol in our blood begins to cause the small blood vessels in the skin to expand. This allows additional blood to circulate closer to the surface, lowers blood pressure and increases our heart rate slightly. This process is what gives us the uplifting warm feeling that makes most of us chatty.

MERRY. (Guidance 6-12 Units)
We soon begin to feel light headed after several more drinks as the alcohol affects our nerve cells all around the body and makes them work a lot slower. Thus our co-ordination and reaction times also slow down, as well as impairing our ability to make decisions.

DRUNK. (Guidance 13-18 Units)
The outward signs of alcohol's effects clearly begin to show after further drinking. Our reaction times become even slower, our speech can slur and in some cases vision can come to be somewhat hazy. Note; If this happens at this level of alcohol intake it's the sign of an amateur - a professional would still be very much at the merry stage. At this point you will have at least a mild hangover to look forward to, and you will have overloaded your liver (typically from 8 units), don't panic! If you take care of yourself in the days that follow it will repair itself. The important thing here is to learn pace; it's crucial to enable longevity. Boost your energy levels by eating (snacking) and consuming booze that utilises energy drinks. You will need to build on this each time you're out, and over a number of years... yes, it does take time and commitment to become a professional drinker.

LEGLESS. (Guidance 19-25 Units)
This amount of alcohol will be affecting cells all over the body. Most amateurs will be staggering about at this level, therefore becoming prone to accidents, injury and fights; usually caused by bumping into someone. Your body will try to clear the alcohol out, as it mixes with the water in your urine in an effort to rid itself of the ethanol. This results in us having to go to the toilet more often, which ultimately leads to dehydration. It is this dehydration that is one of the main causes of your hangover symptoms the morning after; headache, stomach upset, heartburn, sickness and diarrhoea (see The Hangover page 51).

UNCONSCIOUS OR WORSE. (Guidance 26+ Lost Count of the Units)
As a professional you should still be standing and operating in autopilot after consuming this amount of units. Whether professional or not you really need to learn your own limits, you need your body to cope as there's a point at which it can reach lethal levels. Most, if not all, amateurs would be out cold at this point, and even when you're unconscious alcohol in the stomach will continue to be absorbed and can reach a critical point leading to heart failure, reduced breathing, even stopping. Therefore it's important never to leave anyone in this state alone, even if they seem okay they can still be sick and suffocate on their own vomit... not a good way to go!

Government Guidelines
The government advises that if you drink alcohol, there's no safe level. The Chief Medical Officer's (CMO) alcohol unit guidelines say both men and women shouldn't regularly drink more than 14 units a week. [Updated January 2016].

The process.

THE DRINKING GAUGE.

Below is a drinking gauge that shows the complete process cycle of drinking, from your first drink until your last!

The perfect place to be.

THE BUBBLE.

Just past social and prior to danger (indicated in the magenta area of the above gauge) is the key area known as the 'The Bubble'. This is the optimal drunken level with which you should aim to remain at / inside for as long as possible.

FAST TRACK TO THE BUBBLE.

There may be times in which you arrive late to a day, or night, out and need a swift entrance into The Bubble. Your best plan of action is to first purchase two pints, the first of which would be a bitter, better still a stout, something heavy with which to line your stomach. These beers are not to race down in one; it's just that your pace of drinking will naturally be quicker than the friends you have just joined. The second thing to do is to have three shots and drink them consecutively 'A Rally'. They don't need to be full strength just something sweet like Fireball or Sambuca. You could be tempted to go for more but don't do it (save for later), it will only hit you harder and make for an early exit from The Bubble if you go overboard. Shot one is to loosen you up (loosener), shot two is to liven you up (livener) and shot three will get you in The Bubble. It's worth noting that Carbonated (fizzy) drinks speed up the absorption of alcohol into your system and can be used as an alternative. A single shot just to liven you up can often be referred to as an elevator.

THE INNER BUBBLE.

Once you have learnt what this handbook offers, you will develop the ability to drink anything and everything yet remain intact inside The Bubble for lengthy periods of time. However sooner or later, although still standing, your perception, memory, judgment, and reasoning will all slip. Put simply the cognitive processes required for communications as well as responsibility of others in a large group within The Bubble rapidly diminish. This is where you will have friends exiting The Bubble thus leaving more experienced, self-aware professionals using their own volition in converging together to form a smaller and trusted unit that can carry on... this is another level and is referred to as the 'Inner Bubble'. Here, in the Inner Bubble, it can take years to develop the necessary skills as it can still be quite tough communicating. The trick is you have to develop new ways, for example to protest and let your fellow drinkers know you're unhappy with the current bar or club you're in; pour a pint over your head and leave... in short you have to be bold and obvious in your convictions.

Shall we get drunk?

WHY DO YOU DRINK?

Decide why it is you drink and why you wish to become a professional? This is important for not just longevity of a session but your entire drinking career. Ideally it's for fun, bonding and at the most an escape; the freedom from everyday boredom or stress of life, making you feel carefree in your attitude. Good reasons that are at the heart of your spirit within. Darker aspects such as depression, to forget, loneliness and, in particular, if you have an addictive personality are paths that lead to trouble within and spill out into fights and therefore injury and potentially alcoholism. If you're in the latter, your path to becoming a professional is hindered and you should think about being a professional at something else. Don't drink because you're addicted; drink because you're a professional.

III

Money.

CASH IS KING.
Having enough at your disposal is great, if you haven't you ought to think about staying in or see 'cash flow' below for advice. Before you put your money into your pocket you must commit to giving it all up there and then... take it as spent all ready and you're in for no holds barred night.

Once the night is underway, or even before the first beer is sipped, form a kitty as it makes things so much easier. You're more carefree with the cash and it helps with professional bonding as well as keeping the pace up and ultimately keep you going. The person who holds the kitty is referred to as the Ringmaster and will most likely choose the drinks. It will make sense to have some sort of pouch like a material sunglasses case to help keep the kitty separated when intending to get fully intoxicated. If you are the Ringmaster never ask for a tray when purchasing a large amount of drinks, apart from just looking wrong there is a greater risk of spillage and even complete loss.

CASH FLOW.
Young drinkers (professionals to be) may well be a little tight for cash to keep them drinking, but they shouldn't feel downhearted as there are always ways to get drunk. The easiest of which is to mix your drinks. A classic example of this is Snakebite (half a lager and half a cider) or drop a shot of vodka into a pint of lager, or cider. This will soon give you a feeling of happiness and you'll be on your way. If you only have a enough cash for a few shots then drink them through a straw as it has a much stronger effect.

Alternatively, you can 'Load Up'. The concept of loading up is to down a number of shots. Ideally drank consecutively, or extremely close together and continuing on with beer or wine thereafter at an easy pace. Your drunkenness will be strong and will last the night. The secret to successful loading is learning how many shots and with which spirit works the best for you. You could also invest in a hip flask to take out with you in order to save cash. For pre-loading (drinking prior to leaving home) have a beer and use vodka as its impact has a delay of about 20 minutes.

As a last resort, 'Mindsweep', this is going round and polishing off people's discarded drinks... it's all good training but this is perhaps best left to students. However, the alternative is 'Man's Swally' which is ideal for house parties. Locate a teapot, or a jug should a teapot not be available, and basically round up all the left over drinks and pour them into the pot; yes the wine, the spirits, the different beers. It's not for the faint-hearted that's why it got its name!

These techniques do come with a downside in that you're more likely to feel much worse than usual in the morning. For help with this, see the chapter on hangovers for support (page 51).

IIIIIIIIIIIIIIIIIIIIIIIIIIIIIIIIIIIIIIIIIIIIIIIIIIIIIIIIIIIIIIIIIIIIIIIIIIIIIIIIIIIIIIIIIIIIIIIIIIIIIIIIIIIIIIIIIIIIIIIIIIIIII

Bar staff.

YOUR LOCAL.

This is not just your local village pub; it's any of the pubs, bars, clubs you frequent regularly. You need to introduce yourself, individually and as part of a united group and spend time to get to know the staff and have them on your side. Simply buy them a drink. In fact buy a few drinks at the same time and have the drink with them... share the love. This achieves a great atmosphere, quick service, cheeky service after closing, credit, free or heavily discounted drinks and most importantly support and forgiveness for when and if things go wrong (see the chapter on Mischief, Mayhem and Injury on page 43). It's all about fun and loyalty... it makes for first class / VIP drinking.

OTHER PEOPLE'S LOCALS.

Here can lay pitfalls and potential injury, the rules for other people's locals have never been so important. The key here is to start in there early and spend, spend, spend. Staggering into a pub or bar you've never been to at a professional level of drunkenness doesn't go down well... you'll infuriate the locals and have no support from the bar staff or landlord / landlady!

It's not ideal, particularly if you enjoy drinking games (see the chapter on Games page 35) you're liable to cause offence that will result in altercation and injury quite quickly.

Drinking the right way.

GETTING THE BALANCE RIGHT.

It's easy for just a short night out; you just don't go too crazy early on by having half a dozen shots as soon as you walk into the pub. However, if you're out for the day or away for a weekend or longer then you need to drink in the right way. This protects you and keeps your eye on the goal, which is to last as long as possible; 'the long game'. More importantly it's about keeping within The Bubble for as long as possible (see The process on page 28). When feeling on the verge of legless you should stop, or choose your next drink wisely until that passes. You don't want to be keeling over and missing out, it's learning the right pace you need as an individual and as a group that is required for a twelve, twenty-four hour and weekend session. There are additional elements that test you, such as not having enough sleep, to sleep avoidance; Jägerbombs are a good solution for this.

CODE OF CONDUCT.

You need to look at yourself objectively; what kind of drinker are you and how you behave when you're drunk. Understand how alcohol changes your personality and how you impact others around you, both positively and negatively. This is not so you hold back you just need to focus on being a happy drunk, easy going, affable and generous. There is no good place to be found for an aggressive, or indeed sad drunk.

||||||||||||||||||||||||||||||||||||||||||||||||||||||||||||||||||||||||||||||||||||||||||||||||||||||||||||||||||||||||||||||||||||||||||||||||||||||||||||||

DRESS CODE.
You should aim for smart casual; this is for flexibility as it allows for impulse or ease into different environments, the wrong clothes can be an immediate limitation to what venues you can go to. It's also good idea to dismiss things like coats, hats (Trips Abroad exception see page 34), car keys, watches, umbrellas etc. you just don't want, or need, the responsibility. Your phone is important for emergency calls and recording the events of one's night. For or a guy you should always look to wear a belt (no explanation, it's just a rule)… limit the baggage!

UNITS.
Many amateurs believe units to be an exact science, but they're not. They are simply for the purposes of guidance only as there are so many variables from what you drink, to how you drink, to body mass index. All you can do is use it as a gauge to get to know your body. Example: You go out and wake up feeling rough with a poor memory… try to go through your drinks, say you had ten pints and ten shots, (about 30-35 units) and the week before you had a great night and had half the amount of shots, this will help over time to give you indications where your tipping point is for being out of control bordering on keeling over. Remember this is only an indication as food, sleep and length of the session are also factors too.

THE POWER NAP.
This is not ideal, always aim to keep awake as no professional wants to be missing in action. But, as per the chapter 'mischief, mayhem and injury' which will cover eating, if it helps for longevity of the night it's so much better than dropping ninja dust and disappearing altogether. One solution is to miss a drink, again not ideal and you'll get stick for this. Your body has got to be in tune, if it happens regularly then your wish to be professional is out of reach. The other solution as previously mentioned, is Jägerbombs or any drink that utilizes an energy drink to perk you up. If all else fails and a nap happens then at least there is be humour to be had; see Human Buckaroo on page 42.

STRONG BEER.
These are a bit of a grey area, and very much depends on the professional. I prefer standard strength crisp lagers when mixing with all other drinks and find stronger lagers make for a more moody, lethargic experience as well as a much stronger headache in the morning, and you always tend to find you have really thick gunge in your mouth. Remember the art of being professional is the long game. You need to find your starting drink that suits you with the exception of certain situations where you just have to deal with it.

PINTS VS SHOTS.
Normally on a night out you'd be drinking beer for several hours before stepping it up by having a number of shots to get to another level of drunkenness. Be on the ball here as some shots can hit you quick and others take their time to sink in, so depending on the quantity and speed you consume, you can easily over shoot it, too many: too soon could

||||||||||||||||||||||||||||||||||||||||||||||||||||||||||||||||||||||||||||||||||||||||||||||||||||||||||||||||||||||||||||||||||||||||||||||||||||||||||||

ruin you. It's very hard to limit the shots, you can make the rule for limiting shots to three, and this is great until you've had three. Once you've had them you'll want five! So your rule has changed in a blink of an eye to the three shot five shot rule... but once you've had five you'll just want more. I'd go with three to five shots then leave it for 45 / 60 minutes then have a mixed drink like a Jägerbomb or a cocktail (see the chapter What Would You Like To Drink? page 59). Then leave for a while again before having some more shots. Sure you can go crazy and binge on a stack of shots all in one hit and have a short euphoric time, but your night overall is scuppered. Even if you keep going, memory loss will take route and any long-term fun will be lost.

HALF PINT.

Don't do it, just don't. If you need convincing pour yourself a half and go and stand in front of a mirror and take a good long, hard look at yourself.

NOTE: This of course is not applicable when drinking abroad where you have no option of a pint or equivalent large glass, but you should be having two at a time.

LAGER TOP.

This drink is a no go... totally unprofessional if you are out to get drunk, and there is no recovery that can be made from this. Lager top is of course a sign that you simply don't like lager (why drink lager then?). However, more importantly it's symbolic in opposition to that of being a professional and what being a professional is all about. This is not to say that other forms of lager top are not acceptable... for example; A turbo top / turbo shandy, this is lager with Smirnoff ice added or you could just drop a shot of something into your pint, this is known as a Depth Charge.

In fact the lager top is so anti-professional that, when faced with someone in your group making a request for the drink, blank them, or at least ask them to get their own drink and leave the group while they consume it. Whatever the counter argument is, in simple terms it's diluted lager and you may have to start to think about distancing yourself as the great work you have achieved to become a professional will start to become tainted. At this point buy them a copy of this handbook so they can either become professional, or at least understand how not to embarrass you or show disrespect in such a way, ever again. If all fails, terminate the friendship.

Such is a professional's commitment to this issue that if you work behind a bar and have this drink requested you must refer to it as a shandy.

NOTE: There is nothing wrong with shandy, it's an honest drink and has its place; it's refreshing and one or two (max) can help you to get back on it following a big night out.

THE CURVEBALL.

Having the kitty can be a responsibility but it can also be fun; like throwing in a curveball. The curveball is either an unusual, or newly discovered, drink that has a strong foul taste that in any group of drinkers can separate the wheat from the chaff. Try neat Wray & Nephew white over proof rum or Stroh as these are both good choices.

||||||||||||||||||||||||||||||||||||||||||||||||||||||||||||||||||||||||||||||||||||||||||||||||||||||||||||||||||||||||||||||||||

THE GOOD, THE BAD AND THE HORRENDOUS.

You need to identify the one alcoholic beverage you can't drink. This is not a drink you simply don't like, as a professional you have to go with the flow and have drinks you don't like and try new things all the time. What you really need to do is accept and understand the drink or drinks (No more than three or you can never be professional) that you body really reacts badly to. I have drank many a tough drink from Stroh 60 (60%) to 96% proof stuff from Cyprus that's better at cleaning brushes than drinking, but the one drink I can't get on with is tequila… that's my nemesis.

Once you know the drink, don't discard it out of hand or it will bite you when you least expect it. You need to deal with it. To get you on your way play games like the worse drink possible (see the following chapter; Games) and don't shy away from mixing it with other spirits or just face your nemesis head on. Don't just neck it out of hand though as you may well bring it back up, pause momentarily just to prepare your mind and stomach. If this fails you, grit your teeth and just get rid of it, that's drink it, not tip it away! I have a theory, one that I practice, that if I continue to drink tequila one day I will actually like it... worm included! This may never happen but it is the mindset you need to become a professional.

TOO MUCH.

Like any mix of professionals there are always going to be ones that are really in peak condition and really up for 'getting on it' more than others. These individuals usually take charge of the kitty (The Ringmaster). They also, often by default, become the The Mopper, the one that supports fellow professionals that may not be quite on form and will down any residue of alcohol that may be left lingering in a glass by others… Full house!

TRIPS ABROAD.

A relaxed approach is required, you need to look to 'get on it' right away but make things as easy as possible; always have a kitty, always drink the local or national beer/spirit and all drink and eat the same. To avoid upsetting the locals full or part fancy dress always goes down well as it makes it clear that your intentions are just to have fun. Most warm European cities have narrow streets whereby drinkers spill out from bars, something as simple as all wearing the same hat such as a trilby will help you to keep track of one another. In heavy crowds start up the Conga and you'll be able to weave your way through the crowds with ease, you do need to commit to this fully for it to work.

TRIP RECOVERY.

After several days of drinking you simply cannot expect your body to feel good. It takes time; sometimes it takes the same amount of days to recover as you've done drinking. Ideally use your last day to slow your pace. Thereafter relax as much as possible, drink plenty of water and eat as much of the foods mentioned in the hangover chapter (see page 51) over the days that follow.

||||||||||||||||||||||||||||||||||||||||||||||||||||||||||||||||||||||||||||||||||||||||||||||||||||||||||||||||||||||||||||||||||

GAMES.

The great man is he
who does not lose his
child's heart. ~ Mencius, Book IV

Let the games commence.

DRINKING GAMES.

Drinking is a relaxed, leisurely pursuit, either by way of social interaction with friends, or by way of celebration, throughout many countries in the world. Yet here in Britain we have seen how our history has a love of alcohol, a large portion of society actually sees drinking as a sport with competition amongst our friends and piers. There is no doubt this is why we have so many drinking games and challenges, some having been with us for many years, with plenty of new ones all the time. Many of these games are played during formative years, and at the expense of an individual who has to drink a vile concoction or drink at speed. These early games are a good grounding for the future, but as a professional you will actually want to drink these vile concoctions or neck them at speed for the sheer pleasure of it. Games for a professional are more collaborative, fun and progressive. I have highlighted here just a fraction covering the old, classics, from solo to team and some new ones for you to try.

YARD OF ALE. (Historical)

The yard of ale is a very long beer glass holding 1.4 litres (2.5 pints). It's usually around a yard tall, most of which is taken up with a long neck that has a large bulbous end and was known as the 'long glass' in 17th Century England where it first evolved. The funnel shape opening was created to stop the ale from spilling as well as slipping from one's hand. A facet allowing barmen to successfully hand a welcome drink to a thirsty stagecoach driver while they stayed seated high up on their coach. The yard of ale was also used for special toasts, so it's of little surprise that drinking the yard of ale in one go became a well-liked drinking feat in draining it as quickly as possible.

HOW TO DRINK THE YARD OF ALE.

The skill to this is controlling the flow of ale, particularly when it gets to your mouth; this is due to the ales speed and volume being obscured by the froth. Anticipation and readiness is needed for the air reaching the bulbous end as it releases the vacuum sending a rush of ale down its long neck with some force. This is the main reason why most newcomers end up covered in beer, providing much entertainment for onlookers. Some say twisting the glass helps, truth is, it's a challenge and needs some practice in getting the right tilt and flow... go on, give it a go!

NOTE: These days it's more popular to shotgun a can of beer. Pierce a reasonable size hole near the base, put it to your mouth, release the ring pull and let the beer rush down your throat. To shotgun a bottle use a bendy straw, bend it right over and hold it to the neck of the bottle and then drink, the air allowed through the straw produces the same rapid effect.

||||||||||||||||||||||||||||||||||||||||||||||||||||||||||||||||||||||||||||||||||||||||||||||||||||||||||||||||||||||||||||||||||||||||||||||||||||||||

FUZZY DUCK. (Classic)
This is a youthful classic. The game starts with someone saying 'Fuzzy Duck' which is then followed on by each person in turn. If someone says 'does he?' The direction reverses and the words are change to 'Ducky Fuzz'. The idea is to keep building up speed until someone messes up and they have to down their drink to much raucous cheering. If anyone says 'does he?' twice in a row it's classed as cheating and they will have to sink their drink.

FLIP. (Team)
This is a good team drinking game. First up you need to split into two even teams, order the same drink for all, usually a pint (if using shots you'll need a rally – that's three shots each). Teammates then line up next to each other and face the opposing team. Someone not in either team (ideally a barman / maid) shouts 'GO!' The first players in each team down their drink(s) and flip (up turn) their glass on the table (or head) before the next team member can start to drink. The team to finish first are of course crowned the winners!

ARROGANCE. (Stepping it up)
What I really like about this one is the ease with which it can be done at any party, pub, bar or club. It also has the potential for a good mix of alcohol and that element of chance. All you need is a fresh pint glass and a coin. You each then pour some of your alcohol into the glass before taking it in turns to flip the coin, if you guess correctly (heads or tails) then you pass the glass onto the next person, and this continues until one of you guesses incorrectly, at which point they have to sink whatever concoction has been created. If the concoction is still intact after a full circuit you could add more alcohol.

To try.

THE JACK.
Remove three of the jacks from a deck of cards and deal. The idea is to pair down your cards until you are card free by taking a card from the right player in turns (2 x Kings for example). It's good fun to jeer 'He's / She's got the Jack' by ACDC at any player who picks the jack during play. Whoever is left with the jack gets the drink, or you can have a different drink per number of players and you choose as soon as you're out, leaving the worst drink for the last player.

EGG BOMB.
If you don't like pickled eggs this one is going to hurt if you become the 'Egg Bomb'. However you will make great entertainment for your fellow drinkers. It's a simple concept; whoever is last to knock back their drink has to eat a pickled egg (usually found in more traditional establishments or you may have to source from your nearest late night fast food joint). The fun part is singing 'Egg Bomb' to the tune of Tom Jones' Sex Bomb; 'Egg Bomb, Egg Bomb, you're the Egg Bomb!'

||||||||||||||||||||||||||||||||||||||||||||||||||||||||||||||||||||||||||||||||||||||||||||||||||||||||||||||||||||||||||||||||||||||||||||||||||||||||

FIREWATER, OR NOT?

A quick and simple two-player game which is a good one to involve a barman. You have six shot glasses three will be filled with water and three with a clear spirit such as vodka. Only the pourer will know which one is which and adjudicate by double-checking each spent glass. The two players will first flip a coin, the winner of this (player one) will request the opponent (Player two) to down one of the shots. Player one then has to say whether they think it is water or spirit, if they are correct player two continues with another shot… if player one is incorrect the players switch, and so on until all the shots are gone. This is also a great one to watch as well as play.

SHORT STRAWS.

One of my favourite examples; Short Straws is a selection of nice shots through to the awful, if you have the longest straw you have the first pick of the drinks, to the shortest who has to drink whatever is left. It's a fun game that also aids the professional process by encouraging variety and tolerance to horrible drinks.

THE NEXT LEVEL.

Pull up a bar stool and take note that the idea behind drinking games are to get things moving, and getting to the next level of drunkenness. Games do start to become more complicated/difficult to set up and organise as you become more drunk. So, to push on, it's usually best to use excessive behaviour alongside humour with a hint of rationale, peer pressure and challenges.

1. On ordering several Jägerbombs the barman/maid advises, 'You can have four for ten pounds,' you respond, 'Ok I'll have 20!'.

2. This a great one, but you need a big kitty. The basic idea is you order your drinks as normal, once the barman/maid has finished serving your drinks if they say, 'Anything else?' you order another round, as long as they keep saying, 'Anything else?' keep going.

3. 'R'nos'. For this you need a well stocked bar. Simply purchase all the available drinks that have r'no in its name or in its pronunciation; Disaronno, Galiarno, Cinzano etc.

4. Similar to the above work through the worse spirits (barman/maid advice is required).

5. Often you will have a barman/maid wandering round the bar with a tray of shots that are usually on offer… take them all!

6. 'Eight more beers.' First person to finish their drink in the group just orders the round in.

7. Turn your back to the bar, scrunch up a napkin and throw it over your shoulder, which ever drink it hits you order… this can be great fun on large cocktail boards.

8. Create new drinks. Example; Malibuca - a mixed shot of Malibu and sambuca

These are all extreme drink ordering challenges and may render your barman/maid with concern. Hopefully by this point you will be up and running with the help of this handbook and be able to respond accordingly; 'It's alright mate/love we're professionals.'

NOTE: *Alcohol taken another way other than orally such as snorting, eye or rectum are all of course doable.*

||||||||||||||||||||||||||||||||||||||||||||||||||||||||||||||||||||||||||||||||||||||||||||||||||||||||||||||||||||||||||||||||||||||||||||||||||||||||||||

Roll up! Roll up!

After the excessiveness of drinking games you should be at a level where sharing nostalgic stories of previous drunken antics is wetting your appetite to be on the look out for any point of humour to be had. This is about the only time lame or pathetic jokes can be elevated to a higher status so you should never be embarrassed, the more pathetic and juvenile something is the better it becomes.

This is a very creative and productive period of drunkenness, full of ideas and fulfilled fun that you hope to remember the following day, and be able to plot your curve of creativity against your alcohol intake.

FIG: 1

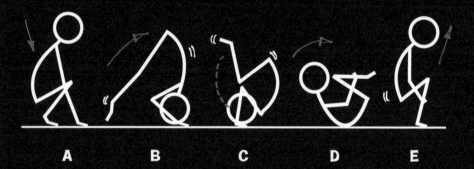

A   B   C   D   E

KNEES IN, HEAD DOWN... THAT'S JUST HOW I ROLL!

Yes the above **Fig 1** shows a forward roll (which can also be done backwards and, apart from great fun when drunk, it's an early lead into a 'Floor Show', a performance that can liven a moment up, generate and project the fun and happy state of drunkenness.

Of course there are other juvenile comedy stunts that you can perform to liven any bar such as the more complicated 'Tanking'! Basically this is a duel forward roll where by you grab each other's ankles and away you go. This is a little tricky to get right even when you're sober so you will need some practicing! Or you could opt for a more simple duel performance such as the Wheel Barrow, Leapfrogging or any combination is good.

More complex or dangerous stunts should be avoided such as climbing and fire (see Other Hazards on page 47), although the Dance of the Flaming Arseholes, in which a length of tissue paper is clenched between the buttocks and set a light, looks impressive. There is of course health and safety issues; with hairy people and it is quite feasible someone watching could die laughing.

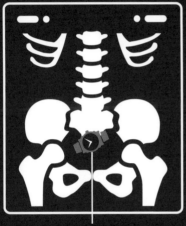

'club was good... we rolled out of there about 4am.'

Don't injest or insert any objects

PRACTISE MAKES PERFECT.

With practice there are more physical or vocal activities such as wrestling, singing or commanding an audience with comedy stories, impressions... even magic. Going nude can produce fun and friction, the former being desired but that's more down to luck than judgment. The point is, if you can't have fun why get drunk?!

The great thing is, immature Floor Shows go down really well, with not only fellow drinkers but even bar staff, owners and bouncers. I'm not altogether sure why, it could be that us Brits as a whole are quite accommodating with drunks (as long as it's not violent) or that the representation, of say, the forward roll is symbolic of 'life's too short, lets enjoy it' and people get that... KEEP ROLLIN', ROLLIN'.

||||||||||||||||||||||||||||||||||||||||||||||||||||||||||||||||||||||||||||||||||||||||||||||||||||||||||||||||||||||||||||||||||||||||||||||||||||

HUMAN BUCKAROO.

This can create entertainment from any drinker who has fallen asleep in the pub or bar. Based on the kid's game from the 1970s in which you take it in turns to try to gently load as many objects onto a spring loaded (pressure sensitive) mule without it bucking (the spring releasing) and scattering the items. With the human version it's all about skilfully balancing as many, or unique, items onto your fellow dunk as possible; such as napkins, straws, beer mats, glasses, bottles, sliced fruit. In a traditional pub setting there is more likely to be ornaments that can enter play, this increases the humour, but be aware if your mate suddenly wakes (bucks) there could be costs incurred for damages. Keep it light and keep it fun, a round of high fives each time an item is placed makes it amusing to watch for people outside of The Bubble.

PERFORMANCE.

If you are not a natural performer you need to help instigate, or at least enjoy the involvement and add to the creativity with ideas. Share in the humour... clap and cheer the classic circus theme "Entry of the Gladiators".

Waking up the next day and thinking 'I don't believe I did that last night' with a sense of shame is no way of becoming a professional; you were drunk, you had fun, let those thoughts go as life's too short.

I could carry on listing so many different games, or comical ideas but there is enough here to give you the idea. It's just about extremes, booze, money, jokes and foolery.

||||||||||||||||||||||||||||||||||||||||||||||||||||||||||||||||||||||||||||||||||||||||||||||||||||||||||||||||||||||||||||||||||||||||||||||||||||

42 | Games

MISCHIEF, MAYHEM AND INJURY.

What is generally referred to as an occupational hazard!

'Don't sip
it, sink it!'

Pubs, bars and clubs.

PUBS.

The pub is your mainstay, the place you most frequent and often start and finish your night in. Here there are casual drinkers and even non-drinkers so it's always good to start early and, just because you may not be advancing to other bars or clubs, don't think of it as a quiet night. Chuck a few cheeky shots in, or some Jägerbombs for good measure.

BARS.

Bars tend to spring up closer to a town centre, have louder music and generally feel at the centre of all things culture wise. They may charge more for their drinks, but it's nice to see all the spirits presented in an inviting way and a better beer selection. As for the cocktails, they are plentiful and it's a pleasure to see them being made. Bars are the sorts of places you just want to live in or take over running yourself. They are buzzing with positivity and fun, even with live music from time to time. Soak this up, this is usually where the night starts when your level of intoxication is rising as you sample the delights they offer. It's crucial to make time for the bouncer on your way in, as by the time you leave you may be sailing close to the wind, you need to be on good terms to allow them to shrug off any misbehaviour your over-zealous drinking has produced. Sure there are other bars, but it's good to have a few that suit you. Location, age group and music; these kind of things play a key part in your bar selection.

CLUBS.

Clubs offer the opportunity to continue to drink. They tend to be noisy and hectic places, so are not ideal when wishing to get to the bar swiftly, or chat. With this in mind, you need to be quite drunk upon entry. If you are in a club and you hate everything about it, you are simply not drunk enough. You have two choices; you either run to the bar and get a series of shots in, or leave. Leaving is only an option if there is another place you can continue on to.

GENTLEMAN'S CLUBS.

If you're a guy, a straight guy that is, it's inevitable you will enjoy these kind of places... we're very visual creatures. However, you need to put this to one side as these establishments offer you your prime target; the continuation of drinking until as late as possible. Ladies, these places aren't as sleazy as you may think and are very welcome to women, some even have ladies nights!

If your partner knows you are professional they will know that the only real reason you have committed to going into these sorts of places is to extend your drinking. Relax and casually refer to it as someone else's idea. Telling them you enjoyed yourself and cheered 'shake them titties', spanked a girls arse or paid for a dance (and of course the female equivalent) is not advised, see relationships on page 58.

II

Curries, chips and kebabs.

EATING AIN'T CHEATING.

This is not only preparing and keeping your body at a good level of food intake to avoid a bad hangover, but it's preventing you from getting too drunk too early. Peaking to soon and before other professionals is bad form. It's also about the long game and staying in the The Bubble. Drinking until sunrise may not always happen, but at the same time you should always try to make it your goal to have a good level of food intake before drinking. Caution; be sure not to get bloated so that you become slow at drinking... no one wants to see a fellow drinker stacking (see appendix).

You need to learn and be in tune with your body. A late night trip to the chippy, kebab house or curry house is what your body needs. It's about the only time greasy food is good for you as the presence of fatty food can significantly slow the absorption of alcohol into the bloodstream. Try a 'Windsor Davis' (see appendix) it's just the job. It's also key to keeping you upright and awake enough to carry on drinking. Relax from the critics on this, if you have a friend that can last all night and not eat, and then wake up right as rain, he's special. Just take a moment, why do you think bars have peanuts, crisps and pork scratchings... salt is good too!

QUEUING FOR FOOD.

By the time you head into one of these food establishments it's usually late at night, unless you are on an all dayer. Be careful, these are dangerous places as so many amateurs frequent them. At the end of the night there are many that have had a bad night, they've been dumped or miserable about something else. When they see the smile of fun on a professional's face they are just itching for a scuffle.

Scuffles and fights.

CUTS, BRUISING AND RUINED CLOTHES.

I'm afraid this is an occupational hazard of professional drinking. As you make aim for being a happy drunk be prepared, as it doesn't always lead to a happy night out. Escalation to confrontation often comprises of miss-judged or badly timed comedy stunts, or it could result from something as simple as bumping into someone. Before you know it you're in an altercation. This is going to happen at some point, it's really only a matter of time so respond positively, apologise and get away from them. If you are at the bar though hold your position, maybe buy them a drink that usually helps. Don't ruin or cut your night short by scrapping over something and nothing. If you have a bouncer charging towards you then surrender, yes literally raise your arms and make your way to the exit, no professional wants to get barred... well not indefinitely.

IIIIIIIIIIIIIIIIIIIIIIIIIIIIIIIIIIIIIIIIIIIIIIIIIIIIIIIIIIIIIIIIIIIIIIIIIIIIIIIIIIIIIIIIIIIIIIIIIIIIIIIIIIIIIIIIIIIIIIIIIIIIIIIIIIIIIIIIIIIIIIIIIIIIIIIIII

As a professional, you need to have a sense of the atmosphere changing. Retaining a small sense of awareness, despite how drunk you are, is a skill. Unfortunately, this skill is not quick to master. It takes time and experience of being in such situations. The alternative is to have a tough as nails friend who can back you up by their presence alone, or a 'buffer', the friend who likes to retaliate and will regularly take a punch. This is ideal, as anything you have failed to pick up on such as a sour situation has been visually brought to your attention by your buffer landing on their arse, thus giving you a chance to remove oneself and fellow professionals out of harms way. At least these episodes are less frequent. Back in the day it was much more volatile when literally everyone had to leave pubs and clubs at the same time! *If you are, or potentially are, 'The Buffer' be proud, your role is key!*

DRINK DRIVING.

Apart from death, serious injury and maybe buggery, this is a professional fear. I'm not sure what advice I can give here since I myself, in my teens, sustained serious injury whilst in a drink driving incident that has left a strong footprint in my subconscious mind. None of us set out, or intend, to drink and drive... the truth is you won't drink and drive until you're drunk. Based on this just plan ahead to make sure you don't have your car keys with you. There is no need to, you're better off getting a taxi (see the section on taxis coming up).

OTHER HAZARDS.

There are many more physical hazards than just that of confrontation, or drink driving. There are the obvious ones such as 'don't run' to risky elements like water; sea, rivers, lakes and ponds should just be avoided. Heights can be another fatal mistake, climbing pranks may seem like fun but usually go wrong. As for balconies, steer well clear of them, they are lethal! Medication is another important one to watch; make sure you read the paperwork or check with your doctor, you don't want your friends thinking you're having a power nap when you've slipped into a coma, worse still choke on your own vomit. Even simple decisions such as deciding to forego a taxi and stagger home on your own has its pitfalls, whether natural or man made, falling down a hole can be painful, even dangerous. So to can cars, if you're intent on staggering down a country lane in the dark know that if a car hits you they are unlikely to stop leaving you to bleed until found which might well be too late; stick to the pavement. While intoxicated you're in a vulnerable state, unfortunately there are people out there who will take advantage of this, leading to opportunistic crime such as robbery or sexual assault.

It isn't just knowing how to avoid trouble, bad decisions or pre-empting possible danger. Unfortunately it's also about observation and experience that brings you better awareness and insight. I have pretty much experienced all of the above in one way or another. In fact I think 95% of my injuries over the years have been drink-related, from stitches to broken bones and teeth.

III

Getting into trouble.

YOU'VE GOT THE WRONG MAN.

Getting arrested is another occupational hazard and a lot of the preventative courses of action are similar to the previous section on cuts, bruising and ruined clothes in regards to awareness. So this is more about how to deal with the arrest. First up, be positive and accept drunken disorderly as a badge of honour. One additional point being; if you're young it's almost as if the police want to arrest you just to get you into their system, so try not to let the natural teenage rebellious streak get the better of you. Charm, and a broad spectrum of humour, is advantageous here, and the challenge is not to be drawn into the police goading and taunting you into an even worse situation than you're already in.

Once in custody, just don't allow the police to twist the circumstances into a crime that is more unrelated such as 'threatening and abuse behaviour'. Say, 'Look this is not me, I was drunk, I was impaired at the time' neither deny nor admit. If you have to plead then remember plead to drunken and disorderly, or at least have this joined as part of whatever else they are planning to charge you with. Why you ask? Well the fact is there is always a hint of an excuse whenever drunkenness is attached to anything, especially if you make a sincere apology. 'I'm sorry, I'm not a criminal I was just drunk' as most people have had a bad drunken moment at some point in their lifetime and can therefore easily relate.

APOLOGISE.

This is key; early in your career quickly learn to apologise instead of being defiant or show disdain it only serves to get you barred which is no good. I use to spend a great deal of my teens going to the pub the following morning to apologise to the landlord... and I'm still apologising now albeit much less frequently. Why? Well, you need to secure future drinking, and to be fair it can be amusing in its own right. Remember the only time you should really be asked to leave the premises is when you're out of money.

BODY ART.

Not to be confused with drawing, say, a large cock (with balls) on your mate's forehead whilst he's passed out, as funny as that is, even with a permanent pen. I'm talking about something more permanent... a tattoo! Subconsciously you may have always wanted a tattoo and just never decided what to have. The moment you're drunk and the opportunity arises, which is usually abroad, you or one of your mates will say 'Let's go and have a tattoo'. Once you're in The Bubble these things happen, and so it's much easier to accept this ahead of time. Chances are if you have one it will only be small, as you will struggle to give up money that could be spent on booze and your window of attention will be limited. So, when you wake up, as long as it is not constantly on show like your face, embrace it. It doesn't matter what it is, or even if it's shit. Like being arrested for drunkenness, it's a badge of honour, and you've had a great night / weekend. Every time you're in the shower you can have a little smile to yourself as you draw in the memories.

IIIIIIIIIIIIIIIIIIIIIIIIIIIIIIIIIIIIIIIIIIIIIIIIIIIIIIIIIIIIIIIIIIIIIIIIIIIIIIIIIIIIIIIIIIIIIIIIIIIIIIIIIIIIIIIIIIIIIIIIIIIIIIIIIIIIIIIIIIIIIIIIIIIIIIIIII

SOS / man down.

KEELING OVER.

Whilst drunk you have to be free from constraints and have the guidance this handbook offers become in-built. You can't be weighed down by feeling it's hard work, and so it's enough to know this moment can and will happen. You are going to have times that you sail close to keeling over or unconsciousness; that's just part of it. It's about testing your limits to find the right balance, basically you will need to make mistakes. For me it's happened very few times. In Kraków, I was up at 3.30am and getting on it for 24 hours. My error was very little sleep, not enough food (see curries, chips and kebabs on page 46) and, crucially, not enough energising with Jägerbombs… just a diet of lager and vodka.

The essential thing is being able to recover quickly. It's not easy and you need some luck here, and this is known as 'the gift'. (Not that you are gifted by the way more that you have been given the gift). I got lucky, after only 1.5 hours down time; I was back on it until 3.30am, continuing the same booze diet. It's almost unheard of and, for me, it has been the only time I'd been this extreme in over 26 years of drinking!

VOMITING.

It is easy for people to make snap judgments and enforce their own drinking rules on vomiting. As a professional, you are more open and accepting of this scenario happening as long as you ultimately try at all costs not to, and part of not doing so is being professional in your approach as it is usually a rule you have discarded that would have been your downfall.

To avoid the mortifying reality of being sick, there are, of course, comedy opportunities such as being sick in a punch bowl. Or, if you're caught off guard by your vomit, you may be in a position to drink it back and therefore counteract the event to some extent.

||||||||||||||||||||||||||||||||||||||||||||||||||||||||||||||||||||||||||||||||||||||||||||||||||||||||||||||||

Ultimately though, your road to, and being a professional will incur vomit. You might be for example, forcing the very drink your body can't deal with or you forget to eat on a 20-hour vodka session. In these situations you are allowed a little leeway. If you're regularly sick and just can't get over this hurdle then I'm afraid your journey is at an end... we can't all be famous, we can't all be professional drinkers.

The taxi.

GET ME HOME.
This is one of the best parts of the night. Despite going home, it's your last hurrah before you put your head down. The humour here can transcend as taxi drivers will put up with almost anything, whether it be floor shows in the cab office, nudity, voicing over the radio mic, climbing in the boot, putting their jacket on. You can get away with so much (they clearly have accepted, or are just use to so much drunken misbehaviour) and for what they charge you... it's a bargain given how late it often is. Don't get me wrong, you can't abuse these cab drivers too much; you have to calm yourself when they reach breaking point with your antics. Treat them how you would your local bar staff (as mentioned previous), you never know, you may really need them one day. So tip them well, and, if you see them during your night out, take time to chat with them, they do a fantastic job! For me the taxi experience could make for an entire book of anecdotes alone.

A note on drugs and sex.

DRUGS MANNN!
Drugs are too much of a personality changer, you'll find, or know, that alcohol brings out your true nature. Mixing drugs with alcohol is, of course, not only dangerous but for a professional it very much ruins the spirit of drinking.

SEX.
Any sexual encounter needs to be taken with an air of caution. Having fumbled sexual intercourse can in itself be amusing and fun, but to have your genitals swell up and weep is not good, let alone creating life! Besides why are trying to pull? A professional is committed to drinking, if by chance it's the end of the night and the bar is closed then that's ok-ish, but there could be fun still ahead as the above section on taxis indicates.

Be positive.

Don't be hard on yourself. Even as professionals, we can all fail at some point; pass out, vomit, urinate oneself and even the extreme of shitting oneself. It's usually down to missing out one of the key steps this handbook offers. The main thing is to not let this hold you back, remember it takes commitment, dedication and endurance.

||||||||||||||||||||||||||||||||||||||||||||||||||||||||||||||||||||||||||||||||||||||||||||||||||||||||||||||||

THE HANGOVER.

'Oh, my fuckin' head... What was I drinking last night?!'

'Hic... just, just one more drink, hic!'

The dreaded hangover.

FEELING AWFUL.

Whether you're an amateur, a trainee, professional or an alcoholic, one thing for sure is that you will encounter a hangover, and you're going to feel awful! Throughout this handbook there is some key advice, but know now that for the hangover, I know of no cure. The search for this Holy Grail of cures can only start with learning how to deal with them, and what I do have is some quick and easy tips you can use to reduce there impact significantly and help you stay as hangover free as possible.

AVOIDING, OR AIDING, THE SYMPTOMS IN ADVANCE.

Hangovers can be quite tough on the body, almost to the point that it can put you off drinking altogether. The two major causes for this are dehydration and stomach acid. This results in the usual symptoms of a headache, often accompanied with stomach ache. These symptoms can range from mild to harsh, which depends on so many factors. Something I learnt early on as a teen, and so began to read, test, create and develop techniques that can help.

Preparation (before you go out)
1. Have a decent meal
2. Drink a good amount of water

'You shouldn't mix your drinks' is quite commonly known and is based on the fact that it's much easier for the body to fight the effect of one lone source, or clean, drink rather than that of many an alcohol mix with more chemicals / substances etc. to deal with. As well as 'drinking clear spirits' as dark-coloured drinks contain natural chemicals called congeners (impurities), which irritate blood vessels and tissue in the brain and can make a hangover worse. Although these are true, it's only to the benefit of amateurs, as a professional must be able to drink anything, not allowing the hangover to dictate what, or how, you drink.

Duration (whilst you are out)
3. Eat where possible; bar snacks and then look to finish the night off at the kebab house.

Other food outlets can be used, but be cautious with curry; too hot and your body will sweat leading to more water loss adding to the dehydration.

Return (when you get home)
4. Drink at least one full glass of water before you sleep as it's the best time to rehydrate, and keep a second glass for when you wake (set this up before you go out).
5. Bread is good to eat as it helps soak up some of the booze and slows its digestion.
6. Have two paracetamol ready for when you wake (set this up before you go out).

It's important to remember that even though you have stopped drinking your stomach is still full of alcohol waiting to be digested and you could in fact peak to your height of intoxication (blood alcohol concentration) whilst you're actually asleep!

Any medical, or dietary advice needs to be checked with your GP or pharmacist.

Some science.

BASICS.

As we move from the preventative measures to the morning after it's a good idea to have a little understanding of what is needed. This can all depend on how you're feeling, what symptoms you are having; bad head, stomach ache, sickness, diarrhoea, tiredness, one, all, or any combination of these (this is why it is so difficult to come up with one easy cure). On a basic level, whatever the symptoms, your body will need fresh air (to bring you round and to clear your head), food (with which to replace the loss in blood sugar level) and, of course, most importantly, water (to combat the dehydration that alcohol inflicts).

So, rehydrating is the first thing to do. Then look for foods that are salty, sweet and full of protein. You can also follow a medicinal approach; painkillers, stomach settlers and effervescent salts (rehydration treatment sachet). Again, you can do one, all, or any combination of these, depending what you have available to hand.

SCIENTIFIC STUDIES.

Since alcohol was first invented, mankind has been on the hunt to find that elusive cure to keep our hangovers at bay, therefore it's always worth keeping up to date with advancements in medical science. One of the most interesting reports I have come across is that Sprite may be one of the best solutions to ease a hangover, as it shortens the duration of alcohol's damaging metabolic rate.

Chinese researchers (Report published in Food and Function 2013) have looked at what actually causes a hangover in the first place and discovered that symptoms such as nausea and headaches could be a result of the body breaking down the alcohol consumed. The liver releases the enzyme alcohol dehydrogenase (ADH) this breaks down the alcohol (ethanol) into acetaldehyde. This, in turn, is broken down by the enzyme aldehyde dehydrogenase (ALDH) into acetate.

Although acetate is deemed nontoxic, the acetaldehyde actually causes the unpleasant symptoms of a hangover. With this information the researchers examined how a variety of drinks (57), affect ADH and ALDH. The result? Well, while some drinks slowed down the process of turning the ethanol into acetate therefore prolonging a hangover, Sprite was found to actually speed the process up, therefore shortening the body's exposure to acetaldehyde thus helping dissipate a hangover quicker. This might also explain why the 'hair of the dog' works by halting the body from doing this process altogether. Asparagus is also said to be good for a hangover according to research by the Institute of Medical Science and Jeju National University in South Korea, as it stimulates ADH and ALDH. Although it apparently works much better when eaten prior to getting drunk.

Almost since the beginning of my drinking career, for me, it has always been about eggs. Interesting in the last few years research has advised eggs too help breakdown acetaldehyde and also contain essential minerals that help rid the body of toxins that build up with binge drinking… So there is the human trial then backed up by research. So keep abreast of science, try things out and most importantly buy some eggs!

Dealing with it.

THE SYMPTOMS AND RECOVERY.

So we have no one pill we can take, but you now have some preventative tips, the basic biochemistry and some science to help you on your way. Now here are three easy steps you can use and develop from the moment you wake up:

1. First thing to do when you wake up is have some effervescent salts; Dioralyte is good.*
2. Have a lemon and lime drink like a can of Sprite or 7up in your fridge.
3. Eat!! Pancakes, poached or scrambled eggs on toast or eggy bread (eggs are high in protein and easy to digest), maybe add a little crispy bacon too. Ideally get someone to make this for you, if not, and you can't face cooking you could try something easy like breakfast in a tin or try a Virgin Mary (Bloody Mary but without the vodka) or my own liquid breakfast 'Back To Life' (see page 68).

Depending on what time you wake you could take a couple of paracetamol first, and you may require additional medication if you have an unsettled stomach. If you do, this needs resolving as soon as possible as you need to eat.

With stomach issues it's still better to eat, even if it's only a bowl of thin vegetable-based broth or coconut water as they're easy on the digestive system. Try some guacamole as avocado is great for the stomach, it acts as an anti-inflammatory and allows you to absorb more nutrients from the food you do eat. If you are in bad way then multivitamin tablets can be an option rather than eating nothing at all. The main thing is to get up and get on with it… the sooner you do, the quicker it will pass and the quicker you can get back on it if you're on a stag / hen do or mate's trip away.

HAIR OF THE DOG.

This will only delay the hangover, however if your on a mates trip abroad then 'the hair of the dog (that bit you)' could be the solution; I find the easiest way to start drinking again is to drink something that is sweet like cider or a Jack Daniels and Coke, Bloody Marys are also good. Once you have had a number of these and you start to feel drunk, you're up and running and should be able to begin drinking whatever you like but just don't forget to eat!

Body and mind.

YOU CAN DO THIS.

Alongside preparation, duration and the morning after you need to understand your body, there are things that you need to try, combine and learn. This takes time and great patience as you measure your hangovers from bad, better, ok-ish to actually feeling better than normal. On occasion you can wake up still drunk which is referred to as The Morning Bubble; you will feel great, yet the hangover will catch up with you at some point. Therefore you need to take the advice here and develop it by finding out what works for you, and create your own concoction of foods, drinks and medicines, as it's quite unique to every individual to get the body semi-functional as soon as possible. However, know that it's not all about consumption... just simply having the right mindset and determination goes a long way too.

AGE AND ACCEPTANCE.

Despite my great work on hangover remedies as a teen, I was pretty poor at maintaining a commitment to following my own advice. This may well be as simple as I'd been binging for so long my body got used to it, and the hangovers didn't seem so bad. On bigger sessions, such as going abroad, I took the determination and endurance option by simply waking up feeling awful, and just getting up and getting on with it as soon as possible knowing that in a few hours I'd feel much better. I'm now at an age where this is tough to do and it's both a body and mind thing. A bad head I can deal with, a bad stomach is the worst, especially if you're on a weekend away and you need to get back on it! For the first time, I have looked and begun to action the advantages of medicine and now have alongside my toiletries, a hangover kit. You have to keep in check with your body and create the solutions on an ongoing basis as they could put you off drinking for good.

As you get older it's easy to think back to your younger self banishing the hangover in under two hours and therefore see yourself as less of a professional. Don't be so hard on yourself for struggling, you also need to take into account that you are most likely drinking more and for much longer than you did back then. Besides, the chances are you have way more responsibilities and therefore not able to lay in bed listening to music all day like you did back in the day.

In conclusion, like most dedicated extreme sports, it gets harder for your body to deal with the hangovers in terms of recovery time as you get older. There is no different a solution for a younger body, it's just a younger body can cope with skipping some of the key points. You therefore must become a lot stricter as you get older and you'll be a lot better off. It's always a good idea to have a clear day following a big night out. Chores, or even having to work will make any hangover ten times worse. Without doubt the hangovers are the biggest threat and have caused the demise, retirement, or at the least semi-retirement of some of the best professionals I've ever had the pleasure of drinking with, and make no mistake my day will come.

DETOXIFICATION.

Beyond the physical and mental effects of the hangover, there is no getting away from the fact you have put your body through an ordeal and potential damage, even if you wake up feeling fine. So it's a good idea (but not essential) to detox by cleansing your body and repair what you can in preparation for your next drinking session. This is easy enough to do, just drink plenty, and I mean plenty, of water. This will purge your body of the bad toxins and will really cleanse your liver and kidneys; you need to look at drinking between 1.5 to 3 litres of water per day. The NHS advises that you wait 48 hours before drinking any more alcohol in order to give your body tissues time to recover, longer if at all possible. You can go a step further by adjusting, or adding to what you usually eat. Don't panic, this doesn't have to be a chore or viewed as a 'diet' as there are lots of foods for you to choose from. Fresh raw vegetables are good for vitamins, minerals and antioxidant pigments to help your liver, opt for vegetable juice for ease. Milk Thistle and artichoke supplements are also good to help in the over indulgence of alcohol. Do your own research and introduce a few recommended foods you like and keep notes in the space at the back of The Handbook.

Memory loss.

WHAT HAPPENED LAST NIGHT?

Time speeds up when you're having fun, from experience a single joke can be moulded and developed to last hours; that's good friendship. We enjoy the tingle phase of a few drinks and the following phase of stimulating free flowing ideas alongside the fun and camaraderie. What's next... prior to the drooling sleep phase, is the amnesia. Your body and mind will use up its reserves for functionality, and default into a state of autopilot. You can keep going for many hours like this and have plenty of fun, however it's the loss of memory that can deflate you, and even defeat you in the morning as great memories of the night really help you psychologically in dealing with a hangover.

So, you went on a lad's weekend and spent twenty hours drinking but can only remember a small part of it, or a big night out leaves you with a scattered memory and unclear events. You may feel disappointment, but you don't need to. Take action; meet up with your friends... my friends and I created **ShandyClub™** were we can meet the following day to chat. This helps piece the night together and bring back those forgotten elements and creates for some professional bonding. Take photos, film, and voice messages when you're out helps. I have often found a video or voice recording days later that has me chuckling, so much so it's makes my day.

Finally, accept that some memories will be lost, ten pints and seventeen shots saw a lost night where none of us had any memories to put together like a jigsaw, or the truth behind the creation of the 'Windsor Davis' (see appendix)... that's just how it goes.

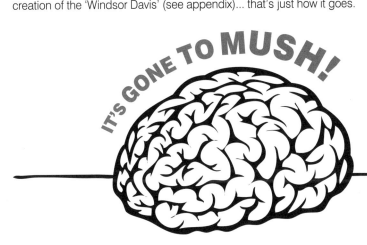

||||||||||||||||||||||||||||||||||||||||||||||||||||||||||||||||||||||||||||||||||||||||||||||||||||||||||||||||||||||||||||||||||||||||||||||||||||||||||||||||||||||

Relationships.

THE START OF A BEAUTIFUL RELATIONSHIP.

There is no question this is a tough area, take it from one who knows. It goes without saying you need an understanding partner. You need to freely admit that drinking is your hobby, your vice, your calling and that there will be mistakes, accidents and let downs on your part from the beginning and that you aim to be a greater partner in every other aspect. This can work, however if you play football, play golf, go to the gym, do this and do that the more chance you have of having a less than impressed partner. It's about quality time and the acceptance that being a professional is about commitment too!

YOU'VE MADE A MISTAKE.

So you are in a committed relationship, but the drink has lead you astray. If this is a regular occurrence it's already a problem and you should feel guilty. If however you somehow stumbled into being unfaithful this will compound your hangover, with what is referred to as 'the cloak of guilt' (see below). Whatever you do don't tell your partner, it won't ease your guilt, it will only increase as you see the anger, or worse, the disappointment in your partner's eyes. You go down this route and your professional career is over. It's either forced retirement or a new partner, it's just not worth it. Your partner will undoubtedly picture a night of passion with someone young and sexy, when in actual fact the reality would probably have been a drunken fumble up against a Biffa bin in a pub car park. You can't remember what they looked like, let alone their name, and you probably can't be sure you even enjoyed it! This is a sorry episode even when single, unless a mate captured it on video thus creating some comedy value.

DEALING WITH THE CLOAK OF GUILT.

You were drunk, you didn't know what you were doing and you wished it hadn't happened... this is what you need to tell yourself and your fellow professionals. Try not to fret too much, the cloak will envelope you and you won't be thinking straight. Just wait, and wait, the cloak will lift and in the long-term you may well learn from it. The alternative is to put it into a box and file it away, in psychological terms it means learn to compartmentalise. Usually described as a negative, as it means splitting your cognition and thinking in two separate areas, especially when they conflict. However, It does allow conflicting thoughts and ideas to coexist by inhibiting direct or explicit acknowledgement and interaction between separate compartmentalised self-states... yawn! Basically it can be a more positive mechanism for dealing with this and other situations such as compartmentalising work from home, so that your home is not tainted by the stress of working. If having parts of your life in boxes is too heavy for you to deal with and the cloak won't lift then share your burden and confess... will you feel better, I'm not sure? Maybe you'll have time to think about this when you end up in a one bedroom flat on your own.

COMMITMENT.

Morals aside, we are but flesh and blood, animals that fornicate and procreate at every opportunity, yet the drink should come first, even if you are single!

||||||||||||||||||||||||||||||||||||||||||||||||||||||||||||||||||||||||||||||||||||||||||||||||||||||||||||||||||||||||||||||||||||||||||||||||||||||||||||||||||||||

WHAT WOULD YOU LIKE TO DRINK?

Here are just a few
of my favourite drinks.

Shots.

SINGLE SPIRITS.

As previously mentioned, shots are a sure fire way to get you to the next level of drunkenness. There is a vast sea of spirits out there for you to try, here I have just mentioned some of my favourites. One shot is 25ml (millilitres) of spirit.

FIREBALL WHISKY

Fireball is a cinnamon-flavoured whisky-based liqueur produced by the Sazerac Company. Its foundation is Canadian whisky. *(ABV 33%).*

JÄGERMEISTER

Jägermeister is a German spirit made with 56 herbs and spices. *(ABV 35%).*

GALLIANO

Galliano is a sweet herbal liqueur created in 1896 by Italian distiller and brandy producer Arturo Vaccari of Livorno, Tuscany. *(ABV 30%).*

SAMBUCA

Sambuca is an Italian aniseed-flavoured liqueur. It's most common variety is often referred to as white sambuca to differentiate it from other varieties that are deep blue in colour (black sambuca) or bright pink/red. *(ABV 38%).*

SAILOR JERRY

Straight-up, no-nonsense spicy rum crafted from a selection of rums distilled in the Caribbean. *(ABV 40%).*

STEPPING UP.

One shot is never enough for a professional, below is a list of drink orders you can place to up the number of shots. **NOTE:** *these are per person.*

2 X SHOTS: THE MICHAEL JACKSON

This is one shot of black sambuca and one shot of white (Black or White). As an alternative you could have an Elton John, which is one white and one pink sambuca.

3 X SHOTS: THE RALLY

This is three shots drank consecutively.

4 X SHOTS: THE DUET

This is both a Michael Jackson and an Elton John.

10 X SHOTS: DEW BOMB

This is purely ten shots, usually based on whichever spirit happens to be on offer.

|||||||||||||||||||||||||||||||||||||||||||||||||||||||||||||||||||||||||||||||||||||||||||||||||||||||||||||||||||||||||||||||||||||||||||||

Mixed shots.

MIXED SPIRITS.

These are the next step above the single shot where you mix up to three spirits, or ingredients, combined to form a stronger concoction that is still housed within a shot glass.

LIQUID COCAINE
Jägermeister and Goldschlager cinnamon schnapps

FLATLINER
Sambuca, gold tequila and three dashes of Tabasco sauce.

JAMMY DONUT
Chambord black, (a raspberry liqueur) and cream, served up in a sugar rimmed shot glass.

BASTARD
Whiskey, with good splash of Angostura bitters added.

STROH 96
Half and half of Stroh and Cyprus 96% (pure alcohol produced by Sodap in Cyprus).

Short drinks.

SPIRITS WITH NON-ALCOHOLIC MIXERS.

Short drinks are served in lowball glasses made with less than five measures of fluid in cocktail terms, but there is no need to get complicated at this stage, opt for simplicity with short drinks. These are a good source of refreshment and a good boast after drinking ten pints or more of beer, or to drink alongside your pint. These are my top five:

JÄGERBOMB TRAIN

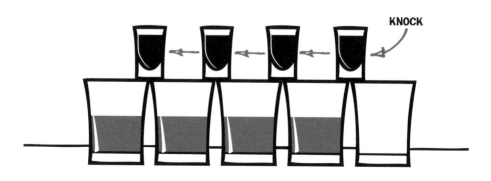

KNOCK

|||||||||||||||||||||||||||||||||||||||||||||||||||||||||||||||||||||||||||||||||||||||||||||||||||||||||||||||||||||||||||||||||||||||||||||

JÄGERBOMB
Jägermeister in a shot glass dropped into an energy drink.

FIRE MULE
Fireball cinnamon whisky in a shot glass dropped into ginger ale.

VODKA & LEMONADE / LIME / ORANGE
Any brand of vodka topped up with a small amount of lemonade, lime or fresh orange juice.

JACK DANIEL'S & COKE
Jack Daniel's or any good American Bourbon whiskey topped up with a small amount of Coke.

JAMAICAN MULE
Pour Sailor Jerry Spiced Rum over ice and top with a fiery ginger beer (carbonated and preferably Jamaican). Squeeze and also garnish with a lime wedge. A longer version of this drink would include Falernum and pimento liquor with crushed ice and more ginger beer, or a ginger mix and lemonade.

Long drinks.

These are drinks that are in highball glasses (about half pint) and from the list above the later three drinks can work well as taller drinks. We also begin to move in cocktail territory, again nothing to complicated here so you should be able to get them down your local pub without too much difficulty. My top five:

GIN & TONIC
50ml London Dry gin
140ml tonic water
1 lime wedge
Fill a highball glass almost to the top with ice cubes, pour in the gin and then the tonic water. Stir well and garnish with the lime wedge.

BLACK RUSSIAN
Originally a 1950's short drink, it has become much more popular with the addition of cola.
37.5ml vodka
25ml Kahula
100ml cola
1 lemon wedge
A highball glass, a little ice, lemon and serve with two straws.

SPRITZER

75ml cold dry white wine
100ml soda water
Slice of lemon or lime
Add to highball glass loaded with ice and garnish with a slice of lemon or lime.

BUCK'S FIZZ

Created at the Buck's Club (London 1921) with a ratio of two-thirds champagne to one-third orange.

100ml champagne
35ml orange juice
1 teaspoon Grenadine
Serve in a wine glass, ideally frosted.

HORNY FROG

Vodka and lemonade has always been a classic, here with the addition of the sloe berry vodka adds flavour and a little more kick.

50ml sloe berry vodka
25ml vodka
100ml lemonade
Slice of orange (wheel)
A wide or conical glass, a little ice and serve with the orange slice (wheel) floating on top.
Created by Mick Franks / Jason Blake 2015

Cocktails.

There are literally thousands of cocktail recipes so I haven't tried the majority of them... therein lies a challenge. However, of the many I have tried here are my top five;

MOJITO

62.5ml white rum
Juice of half a lime (25ml)
3-4 sprigs of mint
50-75ml sugar syrup
1 dash Angostura
50ml soda water
Add lightly crushed mint to the base of a collins glass. Fill up with plenty of crushed ice and a few spent lime peels in-between. Shake the rum, lime juice, Angostura and sugar syrup. Strain slowly into the glass followed with the soda water. Then top up with some more ice, gently stir and add two straws.

FIERY TIGER
25ml Fireball Cinnamon Whisky
25ml Vodka
Juice of half a lime (25ml)
15ml brown sugar syrup
50ml Blood orange juice

Gently shake with crushed ice before straining into a lowball glass loaded with cubed ice and lime wedges. Then top up with the blood orange juice. For a longer drink add a little more juice and for a shooter; rim the glass with lime juice and dip into fine brown sugar, then use even splits of vodka, Fireball and blood orange juice.
Created by Jason Blake 2014, my signature drink.

DISARONNO SOUR
50ml Disaronno
15ml sugar syrup
Juice of half a lemon (25ml)
Lemon twist and cherry

Shake with ice, strain into a chilled cocktail or lowball glass. Garnish with a lemon twist and cherry.

BLOODY MARY
There are many variations of recipe for this particular drink, here's the one I'd go for:

50ml Vodka
Juice of half a lemon (25ml)
6 dashes of Worcestershire sauce
3 dashes of Tabasco sauce
150ml tomato juice
Pinch salt and freshly ground black pepper

A highball glass with a little ice, add the vodka and then the lemon juice, Worcestershire sauce, Tabasco sauce and finally the tomato juice. Give it a good stir and then add the seasoning to taste.

ALABAMA SLAMMER
25ml vodka
25ml Southern Comfort
Juice of half a lemon (25ml)
12.5ml sugar syrup
50ml orange juice

Load a generous amount of ice in to a lowball glass. Gently shake before pouring into the glass. You can also use some of the lemon as a garnish.

|||||||||||||||||||||||||||||||||||||||||||||||||||||||||||||||||||||||||||||||||||||||||||||||||||||||||||||||||||||||||||

Punches and jugs.

There are cocktail recipes that work well in large volume for parties either in punch bowls or large jugs. They are quick and simple and refreshing to drink. Here's my top five:

PIMM'S AND LEMONADE
This is another classic that's great at barbecues and summer parties. The key here is not to skip the cucumber and mint as these make this drink.
250ml Pimm's No. 1 ™
1 litre lemonade
1/2 cucumber, chopped
1 apple, cored and chopped
1 orange, sliced
3 strawberries, sliced
A handful of fresh mint leaves

Mix all ingredients together in a large glass jug. Allow time to chill in the fridge before serving with ice.

STINKY GRINGO
White rum, raspberry schnapps and vodka mixed into a jug of lemonade and garnished with fresh citrus fruits, ideally lime. There is no exact science to the measures here, just as long as the spirits are roughly an even split. Then add the lemonade to taste (dependant on how strong you like it).

CUCKOO ANGEL
This is simply a great drink all year round and I have never met anyone yet who does not like it, which makes it the ideal drink for parties.
4 parts London dry gin
2 parts Lime juice
1 part honey
1 part peach liqueur
Ginger beer

Mix the first four ingredients together in a large jug with ice. Then top up with ginger beer in order to get the ideal taste and strength you're after. Garnish with lime slices.
Created by 45 West / Mick Franks 2016

WOO-WOO

1 part peach schnapps
1 part vodka
4 parts cranberry juice
Lime wedges

Mix all the ingredients together with some ice and lime wedges in a large punch bowl, ladle to hand with glasses pre-frosted if possible.

STRAWBERRY PUNCH

Another great drink for the summer.

700ml white wine
700ml medium red wine
200ml brandy
100ml strawberry liqueur
Juice of half a lemon (25ml)
50ml strawberry syrup
500ml lemonade
Punnet of strawberries halved

Mix all the ingredients in a large punch bowl, add the strawberries and serve with ice. Brandy is not always popular so you can easily replace it with rum if you wish.

Extras.

VODKA JELLY SHOTS.
Jelly spiked with vodka is perfect for parties. Makes 20 vodka jelly shots:
135g pack of fruit flavoured tablet jelly
475ml boiling water
300ml vodka, chilled
175ml cold water

Using a large bowl, add boiling water and the split out the jelly cubes, watching and stirring until they dissolve. Stir in the vodka and cold water and then pour out into plastic shot glasses and place in the fridge for about an hour (or until set).

NOTE: Other spirits can be used instead of vodka, just remember though that these are mini time bombs as alcohol served in this way is absorbed more slowly.

IRISH COFFEE.
25-50ml Irish whiskey
1 tablespoon brown sugar
175ml hot coffee
Whipped or heavy cream

Pour the coffee and whiskey into a tall glass mug, add the sugar and stir before gently floating the cream on top.

JB'S BACK TO LIFE.
If you're feeling rough and tired (hungover) use this booster to bring you 'Back To Life'. The ingredients to this, my (close to) hangover cure, may well look uninviting, particularly when you're feeling rough, but it will do you the power of good. It's much easier to drink than you'd think as all the aroma and taste comes from the citrus fruits… trust me on this.

140-150ml (1/4 pint) milk
1 egg, raw
Juice of half a lemon (25ml)
Juice of half a lime (25ml)
4 or 5 dashes of Tabasco sauce

Give it a good stir and then down it in one. Have another one about half an hour later and you'll be on the road to recovery in no time at all. It's good practice to make it ahead of going out so it's ready and chilled for the morning. If you're feeling confident you could up the recipe to two eggs!
Created by Jason Blake 2009

AT A GLANCE.

An overview.

'Life is
better when
you're drunk!'

At a glance.

PLANNING.

Right from the start have a clear plan of what you want from your night's drinking, where you will go and how long you will be drinking for. Be knowledgeable when selecting your drinks; beer will relax you, wine will cause lethargy and spirits like sambuca will make you cheerful and full of energy. Just remember that if you are up for shots, different drinks will have a different impact on your body, but at same time you need to go with the flow.

DRINKING.

One of the most widely known and common mistakes is to drink on an empty stomach. In addition to this you need to avoid getting drunk too soon, getting in a mess and feeling awful the next day... it's all about how and what you drink. Don't jump straight in with spirits, one shot as a loosener is fine, you're best to start off with beer, continue with beer and drink shots and long drinks as an accompaniment. The trick is to leave spirits towards the second half of the night and not the beginning, and it's a mistake to think otherwise. 'You shouldn't mix your drinks' is a common known fact and if you're an amateur then yes it is good advice, but for a professional no... downing your spirits with beer, or wine, is a sure-fire way to show that you are a professional, or face down in a mess if you're not.

KNOW YOUR OWN BODY.

From the start you need to learn how your body and mind react to different drinks. First understand from a basic level what beer, wine and the four main spirits; vodka, whisky, gin and rum do to you. Be aware of your mood and health. Then move onto different sequencing of these drinks, eventually leading to the introduction of more variety, stronger and exotic drinks. Experimenting and testing drinks on yourself is important as alcohol creates a unique balance in your body, which is why different drinks and the timing of those drinks can have such a different impact. Spirits like sambuca and Jägermeister are the drinks to aim for as they tend to improve your mood and energy, but like all alcohol in large volumes it can cause health issues so you also need to learn your pace and quantity. It's all about being, and remaining, at the optimum level of drunkenness for relaxation, creativity and merriment.

SPIRITS.

Every drink has its own 'speed of effect'. Sparkling drinks kick in pretty quick. Beer is a more stable and gradually lead into drunkenness. If you choose spirits they are more deceptive, vodka, for example, will hit you in about twenty minutes. This gives you a window in which you can drink more shots than you require and will get you in a proper mess. Here The Handbook won't be able to help, your friends are only any good if they're not in the same state, otherwise you're totally reliant on strangers and anything can happen. One thing for sure, your night is over. This makes places like the Revolution bar (vodka bar) a dangerous place with all its exotic vodka flavours that make you feel like a kid in a sweet shop... it's so easy to get carried away.

‖‖

MIXED DRINKS.

Mixing drinks with fruit juices or fizzy drinks may look like you can't take a shot, but the truth is carbonated drinks actually speed up the absorption. It can also be beneficial to mix spirits with a soft drink for your hangover to come as it's predominantly caused by dehydration. With mixers double up your shots!

FOOD.

Start your night out with a piece of gammon (with egg not pineapple), or a nice juicy steak. Don't forget to eat during your drinking session; greasy food slows, and therefore weakens, the impact of alcohol as the fat will line the insides of your stomach shielding it from ingesting too much of the alcohol too soon and knock you off your feet. If you feel you have been hit too hard, in addition to food the best way to deal with it is to move around, walk or dance. Or you could try a power nap, not everyone can do this and recover. After half an hour of activity or complete rest you'll feel much better and should be able to get back on it again. If you have to be sick in order to get back on it you're done, go home and fight to be a professional another day.

HANGOVER.

One thing is inevitable and that is the hangover, it's a part of drinking life and the sooner you accept it and get a plan together the better you'll feel the morning-after. Prevention and remedy is the key to success on the hangover front. The measures you need to take at the end of the night, or early hours of the morning (if you can remember) is to eat as it helps slow down the rate your body absorbs alcohol. Drink plenty of water before you fall asleep and keep a glass next to the bed as dehydration is one of the main causes of a hangover.

Hangovers will vary from person to person, but usually involve a headache, nausea and tiredness. Waking up feeling like your head's going to explode and your stomach is in a bad way, you need a remedy that will get you back on your feet. The advice here is three fold. Firstly; Drink plenty of water. Try a rehydration treatment sachet. Secondly; Medical intervention such as paracetamol. Thirdly; Food. You need to eat right away, try a fry up with a sweet cup of tea. Maybe toast with poached / scrambled eggs, or a particular favourite of mine is eggy bread. If you're really in a bad way and find it tough to face a plate of food let alone cook it in the first place there are a few initial and quicker solutions such as bananas, kiwis, crisps, plain toast or even just bread. It's worth trying my easy remedy cocktail 'Back To Life' on page 68; it tastes better than it sounds... premix and have ready in the fridge.

Whatever you do though, avoid 'the hair of the dog' unless you're on a trip away as it only delays the problem. Over time you will identify what causes different states of hangover and what works for you. Finally take a break from alcohol ahead of your next night out, eat well to cleanse you're body and have it ready!

Follow the drinking guidance here, and throughout this handbook, ahead of your weekend drinking and it will help you have more fun and less pain.

‖‖

GLOSSARY.

Reference Guide.

'Jägerbombs eliminate the need to power nap!'

Appendix.

ABV
An abbreviation of Alcohol by volume and is the standard measure of how much alcohol (ethanol) is contained in an alcoholic beverage (expressed as a percentage of total volume).

ALCOHOLIC
A fucked up professional.

ALCOHOLIC DRINK
An alcoholic beverage that typically contains 3%-60% ethanol, commonly known as alcohol.

ALL DAYER
Drinking that includes all day and into the night.

ANOTHER LEVEL
A successive intake of numerous shots in order to escalate your level of drunkenness to a higher level.

BARRED
The act or being banned from a pub / bar when ones drunkenness has upset the landlord / owner, often it will be for several weeks but can be for life, or until a change of owner.

BEER BELLY
The formation of fat on the stomach, usually happens with age and not down to beer alone, however beer does have a high calorie content.

BEER GOGGLES
Excessive consumption of alcohol can make physically unattractive people appear beautiful.

BINGE DRINKING
Consuming as much alcohol, often as quickly as possible on a night out.

BUBBLE WRAP
Engulfing someone you don't know, or is not really part of your group into your Bubble.

CALLING TIME
Bar is in the process of closing... get in quick.

CASUAL DRINKER
A person that is happy to have a few pints.

DEPTH CHARGE
Dropping any shot of spirit into a pint of beer, ale, stout or cider.

DONE
Completed, finished... 'I'm Done!'

DRUNK
Intoxicated, worse for wear, three sheets to the wind.

DRUNK TANK
Incarceration unit to house those who are intoxicated and being a public nuisance.

DUTCH COURAGE
A shot, or two, of a strong spirit to help relax ones nerves and give confidence.

FIRST CLASS DRINKING
Investing drinks in bar staff and bouncers... easily leading to VIP drinking, discounts, fast service and acceptance, and understanding, of misbehaviour.

FLOOR SHOW
Bringing entertainment to a night out, more expansive on an all day session or weekend away.

GENTLEMAN'S CLUB
A late night drinking establishment that also offers entertainment in the form of gambling, but more often striptease and lap dancing.

GETTING BACK ON IT
Drinking to get drunk following a heavy drinking session the previous day / night.

HAIR OF THE DOG
'The hair of the dog that bit you' is drinking the morning after to relieve the withdrawal symptoms associated with a hangover.

HALF CUT
Half drunk; either at the start, or the morning after the night before.

HAPPY HOUR
A period of discounted drinks, usually during late afternoon / early evening.

HANGOVER
The rough / ill feeling you have in the morning following a big night out on the booze.

HOE IN TOE
When you, or a fellow drinker, brings along their partner to a friends-only night out.

IMPERIAL PINT
British imperial measurement. Many other countries use the term 'pint' but maybe variable in comparison. The American pint for example is 20% smaller!

KITTY
Collective pool of money held by a single person who will order and control the drinks... The Ringmaster.

LAST MAN STANDING
Refers to the last drinker at the end of the night after all others have retired to bed; 'Drink 'till the end!'

LAST ORDERS
Final drinks order before the establishment closes.

LIGHTWEIGHT
An out of form professional who is struggling to handle their alcohol.

||||||||||||||||||||||||||||||||||||||||||||||||||||||||||||||||||||||||||||||||||||||||||||||||||||||||||||||||||||||||||||||||||||||||||||

LIQUID LUNCH
Drinking alcohol during the day at lunchtime.

LOADING UP
The consumption of a number of shots taken consecutively for quick or elevated drunkenness.

MAN'S SWALLY
All remaining dregs of alcohol mixed in a tea pot and then poured and drank.

MINESWEEPING
The process of stealing, appropriating, or simply picking up an unattended or left drink, with the intention of acquiring it as ones own.

MOONSHINE
High-proof distilled spirits generally produced illicitly. Also known as white lightning, hooch and white whiskey.

MORNING BUBBLE
Waking up in the morning still drunk.

NAPKIN
See Done.

NINJA DUST
When you've had enough but can't bring yourself to inform anyone in your group, you just leave when no one is looking.

NON DRINKER
A person who doesn't drink, therefore a person not to be trusted (unless a former alcoholic).

NUDGES
The act of goading someone into consuming a drink by persistently nudging them with it until they drink it.

ONE FOR THE ROAD
A quick drink as you are leaving the pub, bar or club.

ON THE WAGON
A professional drinker who has succumbed to becoming an alcoholic and is now off the booze.

OUT, OUT
Drinking at your local all evening and then going onwards into the town / city for further drinking.

POP
A favourite colloquial term for alcohol.

PPH
'Pints per hour' in terms of how many you have drank, or in reference to how many you are able to drink.

PRE-LOADING
Drinking alcohol at home before going out.

SHOT
25ml of spirit as a single drink or mixed in.

SINCEING
A fellow drinker who has been out earlier and already began drinking prior to the main group.

SOLO BUBBLE
Getting drunk and into The Bubble on your own.

SPLASH AND DASH
Undetected deviation to a far, usually abroad, destination for a drinking session, yet returning home before dawn, or thereafter (without your partner knowing).

STACKING
A fellow drinker who is behind the pace and is stacking one or more drinks.

SWERVING
Avoiding a drink you don't like or missing a drink out.

THE BUBBLE
The ideal zone in which to be drunk, between merry and legless.

THE BUFFER
The person who will take the first punch when trouble arises, giving a chance for the rest to become aware.

THE CLOAK OF GUILT
Shame or guilt that envelopes you the morning after when you recall doing something which is regrettable.

THE CURVEBALL
An unexpected, very strong or exotic drink thrown into the round.

THE DEVIL ON THE SHOULDER
Tipping point of drunkenness where the unsensible side of you kicks in… 'welcome to The Bubble'.

THE GIFT
The luck of a quick recovery after keeling over on a long sustained drinking session.

THE LONG GAME
Using the ability to pace oneself over a longer drinking period than that of just one evening.

THE MOPPER
A professional who's on form and will most often support fellow professionals and down any residue of alcohol that maybe left lingering in a glass.

THE PRE-BUBBLE
Feeling of anticipation and excitement of an up and coming night out on the drink.

THE RINGMASTER
He, or she, who holds the kitty.

THE TIPPER
Not the person who's generous, but one that tips away their alcohol as opposed to drinking it.

WAFT
A gentle waft of the hand to let a situation go, this can save confrontation, injury and arrest.

WINDSOR DAVIS
Protein filled meat only feast of doner kebab meat topped off with a large sausage and chilli sauce; *'Lovely boy, lovely boy', Windsor Davis' catchphrase from the 1970s TV show 'It Ain't Half Hot Mum'.*

||||||||||||||||||||||||||||||||||||||||||||||||||||||||||||||||||||||||||||||||||||||||||||||||||||||||||||||||||||||||||||||||||||||||||||

Drinkware.

GLASSES AND A FEW ACCESSORIES.

It's always good to have a variety of glasses in the home for parties and special occasions, and even better just to simply have the knowledge of some of the key ones.

Conical	Tulip	Nonic	Weizen	Pilsner
- Beer (Pint) -	*- Beer (Pint) -*	*- Beer (Pint) -*	*- Beer (Pint) -*	*- Beer (Pint) -*

Stange	Mug	Tankard	Stein	Pitcher
- Beer (Pint) -	*- Beer (Pint) -*	*- Beer (Pint) -*	*- Beer (Pint) -*	*- Beer (4 x Pint) -*

Collins	Highball	Lowball	Shot	Wine
- Mixed Drinks -	*- Mixed Drinks -*	*- Mixed Drinks -*	*- Spirts (25ml) -*	*- Wine (125 / 175 / 250ml) -*

Flute	Coupe	Cocktail	Snifter	Pokal
- Champagne (Similar) -	*- Champagne (Similar) -*	*- Cocktails -*	*- Brandy / Cognac -*	*- Liqueurs -*

Punch Bowl	Tea Pot	Hip Flask	Thimble Measures (ml)	Cocktail Shaker
- Punches & Cocktails -	*- Man's Swally -*	*- Spirits -*	*- 25 / 35 / 50 / 125 / 175 / 250 -*	*- Cocktails -*

Sign off.

FROM THE PAST TO THE FUTURE.

How To Be A Professional Drinker has been a while in the making as time served at the bar, inclusive of the amateur years, has of course been essential. To what started out, as more of a scrapbook has over time become The Handbook with all relevant, key information and examples that one would need to become a professional drinker is now finally being shared for future drinkers to use and for them to expand upon.

The following pages are designed for you to log your progress in becoming a professional drinker and to note any great drunken memories, games, drinks or ideas.

THANKS.

It now only leaves me to thank you for taking the time to read this handbook and raise a glass to those that have. I'd also like to thank my fellow professionals; Mick Franks, Rich Franks, Nick Giannini and Robin I'Anson for without them this would not be half the book it is.

All proceeds from this handbook will be spent on alcohol. So here is to being a professional, drinker... cheers!

Your notes.

'It's alright mate, I'm a professional!'

'Don't let
The Bubble
burst!'